From Autumn to Summer

Jonathan Magonet

From Autumn to Summer

A Biblical Journey
Through the Jewish Year

scm press

For Doro, Gavriel and Avigail

An earlier version of this book appeared as *Mit der Bibel durch das Jüdische Jahr* (Gütersloher Verlagshaus, 1998)

0 334 02819 1

This edition first published 2000 by
SCM Press
9–17 St Albans Place London N1 0NX

SCM Press is a division of
SCM-Canterbury Press Ltd

Typeset by Regent Typesetting
and printed in Great Britain by
Biddles Ltd, Guildford and King's Lynn

CONTENTS

Contents

INTRODUCTION

The Jewish New Year begins in the autumn. Actually, as with most things Jewish, that is not the entire story, since there are altogether four Jewish 'new years' – but more of that later. However if we are to journey through the Jewish year and stop off to visit certain times and places, autumn is a good season to begin.

Since we are beginning in the autumn, just after the penitential season of *Rosh Hashanah* (New Year's Day) and *Yom Kippur*, the 'Day of Atonement', it is appropriate to begin with a confession. It is about the genesis of this book. The pieces presented here began life as radio broadcasts for Friday evening, the eve of *Shabbat*, for a German radio station, the *Norddeutscher Rundfunk*, and I am particularly grateful to Peter Hertel for inviting me in the first place to do them and for accepting my bad pronunciation of German when I read them. Since I was asked to contribute four times a year, the broadcasts tended to cluster around certain periods and certain readings from the Hebrew Bible. This latter fact may also need a bit of explanation.

The Five Books of Moses are known in Jewish tradition as the *chumash*, from the Hebrew word for five, or else as the *Torah*, a word that will also come to stand for the entire Hebrew Bible and all the religious teachings that will be derived from it. The *chumash* is divided into fifty-four portions (Hebrew *parashiot* or *sidrot*) for weekly readings in the Synagogue so that the five books can be read in their entirety in the course of a single year in Ashkenazi (East European) communities. There is also a three-year cycle used by Sephardi (Spanish and Portuguese) communities while the different Reform, Liberal, Conservative and Reconstructionist Jewish communities read larger or smaller selections from the weekly portion according to their own choice. Since the Jewish Calendar varies slightly from year to year and sometimes Festival days coincide with the *Shabbat,* there are occasions when two sections may be joined together to ensure that all are read during the course of the year.

To each of these '*Torah* readings' is attached a reading from the prophetic books, the *Haftarah,* which in some way echoes one of the themes to be found in the *Torah* passage. It is possible that these readings were introduced at a time when Jews were forbidden to read publicly from the *Torah* on *Shabbat,* so they read instead a prophetic piece that effectively reminded the congregation of what they should have been hearing. (The full list of traditional *Torah* and *Haftarah* readings for *Shabbat* for the year can be found in Appendix 1.)

Though it is not compulsory to do so, it is the traditional practice to preach on the weekly *Torah* reading. One classical method was to start with the most obscure possible verse to be found in the *Haftarah* and by a series of arguments to reach a triumphant conclusion in which the preacher ended by quoting a verse from the *Torah* reading for the week, which by now bore a special meaning because of all that had led up to it. Since few rabbis have the time to prepare such an elaborate sermon, and fewer congregations would appreciate it, most preaching will simply include a verse from the *Torah* and try to apply it to some current event in the life of the congregation or in Jewish life in general. Since not all passages lend themselves to an obvious contemporary meaning, this is not always easy. One set of readings in particular, *tazria-metzora* (Leviticus 12–15), deals with vaginal discharges and skin diseases, so it is considered 'in the trade' as something of a 'rabbi-killer'. Still the challenge to find something relevant to say is half the fun of the exercise! (The attention span of congregations has also shrunk in recent years. In the 'good old days' you could preach for at least half an hour. Today, in the congregations I know, people start to get restless when you get to the twelve minute mark. Of course there are preachers who can make even twelve minutes seem like much more than half an hour.)

For the radio broadcast, I was asked to comment on some verses from the *Torah* passage for the week and occasionally from the *Haftarah* for variety, with the overall aim of trying to say something of interest and relevance to the radio audience. (My favourite version of such requests is the woman who asked the rabbi at the last minute on a public occasion to say something 'brief, profound and witty'.)

Officially this was a 'Jewish' slot on the radio, but I had to assume that most of the listeners would be Christian. (In all the years I have done the broadcasts I have only ever met one person who had actually heard them – or admitted to having heard them!)

When it came to turning these passages into a book form I arranged a meeting with my German editor, Ulrike von Essen. We sat in an outdoor café on the Rhine in Koblenz, on what must have been the last day of summer. (Our first decision was to sit under the trees in case it rained, until we were bombarded by horse chestnuts crashing around us. The book was nearly still-born when one just missed my head, and we decided to risk the rain instead.) What began to emerge as we tried to organize the materials was that they gave insights into Jewish life around the year, but from unfamiliar perspectives. What also became clear was that this would not be a fully comprehensive and systematic examination either of the Jewish calendar or of the entire list of *Torah* readings for the year. Instead the book could only provide a sampling of themes and passages. Nevertheless, I hope that what is contained here will give the flavour both of some current issues in Jewish life and of a particular way of working with the Hebrew Bible.

It will be helpful as a background to have a brief overview of the Jewish year just to show the context in which the chapters of this book operate. Since such surveys are common, I want to offer something a little different. There are many useful books that list the Jewish festivals and fasts as they follow each other through the year. But if you have to live with them as part of your Jewish life, you are soon struck by the odd way in which a lot of them seem to gather together in the autumn months, so much so that it is an annual source of complaint by Jews. It is also particularly tough on rabbis who find themselves organising endless numbers of services and writing innumerable sermons just at the time when they should be finding space for their own self-examination and prayer. The following survey may help to explain how this uneven distribution has come about.

Rather than dealing with a single cycle of events that has been systematically thought through and organized, we have actually inherited at least four full cycles that have their unique origins in different times and places and are overlaid upon each other.

Perhaps the oldest cycle is that of the three pilgrim festivals – *Pesach* (Passover), *Shavuot* (Pentecost) and *Sukkot* (Tabernacles). They were originally harvest festivals in the early and late spring and autumn, accompanied, later, by a pilgrimage to Jerusalem. At some stage an historical interpretation was added to each, commemorating in turn the exodus from Egypt, the revelation at Mt Sinai and the wandering in the wilderness symbolized by living in booths. (The fact that in the wilderness the Israelites are described as living in tents and the 'booth' was actually the place in the field where you could shelter from the sun betrays the real origin of the festival in the context of the harvest). The period between Passover and Pentecost is marked by a formal counting of each of the days and reciting a blessing – the 'counting of the *Omer*' – so that these festivals are formally linked together. This is a period of semi-mourning interrupted on the thirty-third day, *lag ba-omer*, on which marriages may be celebrated.

The Jewish calendar is so arranged that these festivals fall at the approximate time of the year when the respective harvests would happen in the land of Israel, a brilliant bit of Rabbinic mathematics that ensured that the 'reality' of life in the land of Israel was maintained even though the people lived far away in exile (see Figure A).

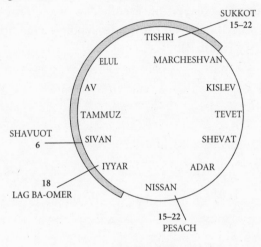

FIGURE A

The second cycle is that related to the 'High Holydays' around the autumn New Year. The 'Day of Atonement' is mentioned in the Hebrew Bible, the 'tenth day of the seventh month', together with the elaborate rituals of the high priest to remove the sins of the people from the encampment. (By the way, for this to be the 'seventh month' assumes that the year was also regarded for certain purposes as 'starting' in the spring at the time of the Passover which occurred in the 'first' month, *Nissan* – Exodus 12.2.) Curiously, though the first day of the seventh month is mentioned as a festival day, no particular significance is given to it (Leviticus 23.23) and it is the rabbinic tradition that fills out the

details of its importance as *Rosh Hashanah*, New Year's Day, the
day which was the 'birthday of the world' and on which God
judges the world each year. Theirs too was the addition of the
previous Hebrew month of *Elul* to the 'penitential season' as a
time of preparation. A *shofar*, ram's horn, is blown daily during
the month to call people to repentance. This penitential cycle
does not end on *Yom Kippur*, the day on which God closes the
'Book of Life' having made the judgment, but on a day called
Hoshanah Rabbah, actually the seventh day of the festival of
Sukkot, when the 'Book', according to rabbinic tradition, is
finally sealed (see Figure B).

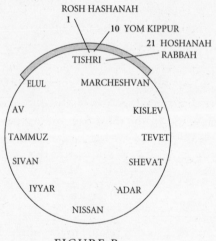

FIGURE B

The third cycle that we must superimpose occurs mostly in the
summer, but also continues into the autumn. It surrounds the
events leading up to and following the destruction of Jerusalem
and the Temple in the biblical period and again centuries later
during the Roman period. A series of fasts marks the stages of the
assault on Jerusalem. On the tenth day of the month of *Tevet* the
siege of Jerusalem by Nebuchadnezzar, King of Babylon, began.
The seventeenth day of the month of *Tammuz* was selected to
mark the day when the walls of Jerusalem were breached. Three

weeks later on the ninth day of the month of *Av*, Solomon's Temple was destroyed, and Jewish tradition records that not only was the Second Temple destroyed on the same day by the Romans, but that any number of other disasters that befell the Jewish people happened on the same date.

During the three weeks leading up to this day, known as the 'black fast', the prophetic readings on *Shabbat* contain solemn warnings about the destruction to come. However from the Sabbath following the ninth of *Av*, the readings from the later part of the Book of Isaiah are words of consolation, ending just before the New Year itself, offering comfort and support as we enter the time of penitence and judgment. But this cycle does not quite end there. One consequence of the conquest was that the Babylonians appointed a governor over the country, Gedaliah. But he was assassinated by someone who presumably regarded him as a traitor and that day is also marked by a minor fast, the Fast of Gedaliah, which occurs on the third day of the month of *Tishri*, that is to say, the third day of the New Year, right in the middle of the Ten Days of Penitence, thus adding one more element to the complexity of that period (see Figure C).

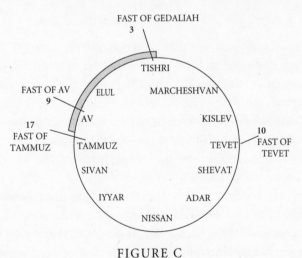

FIGURE C

The fourth cycle is the one which is directly related to the subject of this book – the weekly reading of portions from the *Torah*, for the completion of the reading of Deuteronomy and the beginning of the reading of Genesis are celebrated with the festival of *Simchat Torah*, 'The Rejoicing in the Torah', which comes at the end of the Festival of *Sukkot* as a climax to this complex period.

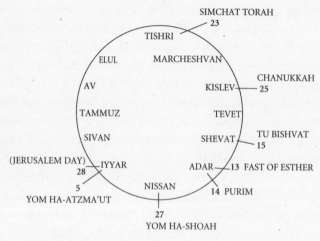

FIGURE D

For completeness we should add two other traditional 'minor' festivals: *Purim*, in the early spring, that celebrates the rescue of the Jews of Persia from the genocidal plans of Haman, vizier to Ahasuerus, the King of Persia, as recorded in the Book of Esther; and *Chanukkah*, the Festival of Lights, at the time of the winter solstice, which records the struggle of the Maccabees against the Syrian–Greek empire and the rededication of the Temple in Jerusalem.

It is rare that a new festival is ever added to this calendar, but the rebirth of the State of Israel led to the declaration of Israel Independence Day as such a day. It occurs in the middle of the *Omer* period, again transforming a period of semi-mourning into one of celebration on that particular day, the fifth of *Iyyar*. More tragically, various days are selected to mark the genocide of the Jewish people in the Nazi period. Of particular significance is *Yom Ha-Shoah*, the twenty-seventh of *Nissan*, a day that falls within the period of the Warsaw Ghetto Uprising against the Nazis. Another day that is commemorated is the 9th of November, the date of *Kristallnacht*, when Synagogues throughout Germany were burnt to the ground in 1938.

To the above descriptions should be added, of course, the greatest 'festival', namely the *Shabbat* itself, with its weekly taste of the peace, rest and perfection that await the world in the Messianic time. The New Moon, *Rosh chodesh*, literally, 'the head of the month', is celebrated as a minor festival, with special additions to the daily service. According to an old tradition, women ceased from work on this day and this has led to the adoption of this Festival by the women's movement in recent times.

In preparing this English edition, I have added new broadcasts that have been made in the years since the German original appeared and adjusted some things that are too geared to a German audience. The appearance of this edition affords me the opportunity to express my gratitude to John Bowden, my editor for four previous SCM Press books, who undertook to oversee this book as one of his last tasks before retiring from the Press. The remarkable output of significant works of Christian theology under his stewardship of the Press, as well as his no less phenomenal translations of significant (and long) works of German scholarship, would earn him a place in any publisher's heaven. But no less significant is the opportunity he has given to Jewish writers on religious themes, in particular men and women rabbis, graduates of Leo Baeck College. It has been a privilege to be one of his 'authors'.

Writing these broadcasts is always a challenge, but also great fun. The given is a biblical text anchored in a particular time and place that has somehow still managed to stimulate, influence or disturb people for over two millennia. Like generations of rabbis before me the task is to try to be true to the biblical text but also true to the needs of today, to be a bridge to the past but also to move on our thinking or imagination. As with all my books on the Bible, I hope it will stimulate others to work with the texts to find a way of applying them to today's issues without either completely distorting the text (a little distortion is to be expected – this is called 'rabbinic licence') or being less than honest to the problem being addressed. The rabbis said: 'turn [the *Torah*] and turn it again, for everything is in it', but also warned: 'do not use [the *Torah*] as a spade to dig with'. Somewhere between letting the Bible speak and exploiting it lies the delicate area of applying scripture to life. I hope the following passages successfully tread this middle ground.

THE JEWISH CALENDAR

(*Ki Tavo* Isaiah 60)

As autumn begins and the days grow shorter we become more aware of the passing of time. The Jewish community begins to look inward as the great autumn festivals approach – the High Holydays with their themes of repentance and atonement; the festival of *Sukkot*, Tabernacles, the time of harvest and a period for contemplating the transience of life. In these days we become very conscious of the passing of time and it may be helpful to look at how we understand it and seek to control it.

The way that we measure time reveals much about our human concerns and values. The very numbers that we use to measure time remind us that this is a very ancient issue. Why are there sixty seconds in a minute and sixty minutes in an hour? Because the number sixty is at the heart of a numerical system in use by the ancient Babylonians. In fact it is a system so old that it is taken for granted by the compilers of the Hebrew Bible so that the number sixty and its multiples occur very frequently.

But as well as counting and measuring time, we also make value judgments about it – dividing it up into years, epochs, dynasties, millennia as ways of orientating ourselves in the world. Even the way we number the years is an attempt at establishing a kind of ownership over them. In the Jewish calendar we are in the year 5761 (= 2000 CE) since the creation of the world – calculated on the basis of the dates given in the Bible. The Christian calendar orientates itself around the birth of Jesus, to express their faith in the transformation of the world through his life. Muslims also have their way of dating so as to establish the new epoch that began with the advent of Islam. Time in this particular sense is not neutral. Rather it is placed very firmly under human control.

Smaller units of time are also measured. In Europe we are used to dividing up our year according to the seasons, so that the rhythm of nature helps us orientate ourselves. But a whole variety of artificial moments also colour our seasons. We have a new year celebration on the first of January, but we know other 'new years' as well, each with a different emotional content. The academic year runs from the autumn and brings a special kind of excitement to this period. The Income Tax year runs from April, and that gives us an entirely different kind of feeling when the first spring flowers begin to appear. Jewish tradition speaks of four new years – the Spring New Year is the one for measuring the reign of kings and the festivals of the year. In the time when the Second Temple stood the rabbis described a new year for the planting of fruit trees and another one for assessing the gifts that were to be donated to the Temple.

Each of these new years, whether secular or religious in character, affects our understanding of the nature of time. But there are even smaller units that have their impact on the way we think and feel about our life and its meaning. Judaism, in particular, puts its stamp upon whole periods of the year. The four *Shabbats* before the festival of *Pesach* (Passover) are marked by special readings which prepare us for the arrival of the festival. But the seven weeks between *Pesach* and *Shavuot* (Pentecost) known as the period of the counting of the *Omer*, are days of great solemnity and semi-mourning. Only one of them, *lag ba'omer*, the thirty-third day of the Omer, breaks this pattern and is set aside as a day to celebrate weddings and happy events. Even the end of that period has special significance.

Seven days before *Shavuot* we celebrate for two days the beginning of the New Moon. The last three days before *Shavuot* are days of preparation for the Revelation at Mt Sinai that is about to be commemorated. But that leaves one spare day between the end of the New Moon celebration and the preparatory days before the festival of *Shavuot*, so it is also given a special title – it is called *yom di miyuchas*, which means 'the day of connection' – and it is given a special name precisely because nothing special happens upon it! Even unmeasured time takes on a meaning when the calendar is so filled with special events.

Another sustained period of time that affects our way of seeing the world occurs over the summer. The central factor is the ninth day of the Hebrew month of *Av*, the black fast known as *Tisha b'Av*, which commemorates the destruction of both the first and second Temple and many other disasters in Jewish history. It is preceded by three weeks that correspond to the period of the siege of Jerusalem and the breaking down of its walls, so all festivities are deliberately avoided in memory of those events. The *Haftarot*, the prophetic readings, on the *Shabbats* during this period are called the '*Haftarot* of Rebuke'. They contain the warnings of the prophets Jeremiah and Isaiah about the destruction to come, and call the people to change their behaviour and turn back to God. If these are times of national mourning for past failures, the *Shabbat* after *Tisha b'Av* is called the 'Sabbath of Consolation' when we hear the words of the Prophet Isaiah (chapter 40) bringing comfort. He tells the exiles in Babylon that their time of exile is over and their restoration is about to begin. In fact the next seven *Shabbats* after *Tisha b'Av* all come from Isaiah and contain this same refrain, so that they are known as the Seven Haftarot of Consolation.

Today's *Haftarah* is the sixth of the series and next week's, the final one, is the *Shabbat* before *Rosh Hashanah*, the New Year. This suggests that we enter the time of repentance and forgiveness and atonement, strengthened by the promise of God's love.

Today's *Haftarah* is joyous in its promise of restoration. God speaks directly to Jerusalem:

> Rise up, shine, for your light has come, the glory of the Eternal has risen upon you ... Nations shall walk in the light that comes from you. Your sons and daughters who have been scattered to the far ends of the earth are returning to you. Nations shall come flocking to you as well. Foreign peoples shall build your walls; they will make your sanctuary beautiful again. The sons of those nations that destroyed you shall now come and bow down before you, bringing with them the wealth of their lands.

To this picture of the joyful return of Israel to Jerusalem, and the pilgrimage of the nations, is added an even greater promise for all peoples:

> Violence shall no more be heard in the land, no more desolation or destruction within your borders. (v 18)

This vision of hope and joy helped sustain the Jewish people through two thousand years of exile. But as I have suggested, it does not stand alone, but as part of an entire calendar of fasts and festivals, special seasons and days, serious and comic, sad and joyful. To experience the promise and hope of this *Haftarah*, we have to have known the bitterness and sorrow of *Tisha b'Av*, and felt the loss of the Temple and all the other destructions that have befallen us. That is to say, we live out a year of feelings and emotions that run parallel to the realities and conventions of our everyday life. We experience two kinds of time at once – the timeless pattern of life of the Jewish people and the timebound pattern of our own days.

Of course, there can be a great tension between these two senses of time. If we live wholly within the tradition, it is possible to feel completely at home within the religious calendar. But most of us find ourselves living in normal secular time, only able occasionally to make the emotional and imaginative leap into the Jewish calendar in its totality. Since we cannot do it unselfconsciously, we have to work very hard at it. It is rather like the preparation done by 'method actors'. In order to portray the emotional life of a particular character, they try to contact some past emotion within themselves that they can remember. They search into their childhood experiences of loss or love or embarrassment or anger – and if they can capture the emotion, then their own creativity and imagination and intuition can take it further until they enter the skin of the person they are portraying.

In the same way we who begin to approach the Jewish calendar, and indeed every other aspect of Jewish life, from the outside, from the margins, must try to get beneath the surface, of ourselves and of the festivals, till we can find the point of linkage and work from there. There are no guarantees that such a process will be effective, but sometimes the outer and inner reality coincide. Then we begin our own version of that strange dance between the different realities that make up our own life; between the tradition and the new; between our particular identity as Jews and our universal identity as human beings; between the faith that illuminates the history and experience of our people, and the small, uncertain faith that is often all we have to guide us in this secular age.

It is a difficult journey into our Jewish world. And sometimes it is easier to commemorate the sad occasions, the memories of Jewish suffering and disaster, than to understand and experience the joy. Perhaps sadness is a deeper emotion and joy too ephemeral. It cannot be willed into being, or perhaps we are too self-conscious to let it grow. And yet we would not be true to the tradition if we let sadness dominate our Jewish life. Every *Tisha b'Av*, every time of mourning, is followed by its *Shabbat Nachamu*, Sabbath of comfort and consolation. Time is not empty nor of a single colour alone – it carries the emotions and colours that we will it to have.

Even the great cynic Kohelet, Ecclesiastes, recognized that we have to struggle with time, to carve a meaning out of its endless cycles and repetitions. His are the famous lines:

> To everything there is a season and a time for every purpose under heaven ... A time to weep and a time to laugh, a time to mourn and a time to dance. (Ecclesiastes 3.4)

God does not cheat – all things come to us at some point in our lives. So all must be faced or valued in their time for what they are, as stages on a larger journey.

Our Haftarah reminds us that now is a time for joy and hope – Jerusalem may yet become a centre of peace for all the nations of the world, when

> Violence shall no more be heard in the land, no more desolation or destruction within your borders (Isaiah 60.18).

An Afterword – Jerusalem

June 1st

The calendar maker
awaits only
a date
a result
to declare
the new festival.

A day of joy?
A fast?
Who
and where
to celebrate?

He hesitates –
the calendar is full
the balance almost perfect
so many still to add.

The sightless beg
just one more shade
and with a shrug
he writes.

June 7th

Two stars
darkening rainbow sky
pink-rimmed Jerusalem hills
a cricket
distant gunfire
blood on my white coat.

                    Jonathan Magonet

AUTUMN

WHAT'S IN A NAME

(*Lech l'cha* Genesis 17.1–2)

I was given two names when I was born. One I use for my everyday life. The other one is my Hebrew name. It is only used on certain religious occasions, such as when I am called up to the reading of the *Torah* in a synagogue. It is also inscribed on my Jewish marriage document. The same is the case with most Jews, though many may have forgotten their 'Hebrew name' if it was given them as a child and never used since.

My first name, Jonathan, happens to be a good biblical one, though pronounced in the English manner. It was only in the Middle Ages, and more particularly in the last few centuries, that Jews have acquired European first names and surnames – often as a result of government decrees to regulate the Jewish community. This procedure has disrupted long traditions of family Hebrew names that were handed down from generation to generation. Not only were family connections kept alive through this procedure, but even traditions about particular members.

Of course this could sometimes lead to difficulties. The story is told of a family that had a major problem. A boy was born into the family, and a debate raged: after which of his grandfathers should they name him – his mother's father or his father's father. The problem was that they were both called Yankel, but while one grandfather Yankel, his mother's father, was a great scholar and saintly rabbi, the other Yankel, his father's father, was a notorious horse thief. Which side of the family should they

honour? Finally, as in all such cases, the family decided to call in
the rabbi to resolve the problem. After which Yankel should the
child be named? The rabbi thought long and hard and finally
came up with the solution. 'You must call him Yankel', he said,
'and then wait and see what happens when he grows up. If he
becomes a great and saintly rabbi, then you know he was named
after the saintly Rabbi Yankel, the father of his mother, but if,
heaven forbid, he becomes a horse thief, then he was named after
the other Yankel.'

I do not know whether I had any horse thieves in my family,
though I certainly had a few rabbis. But my Hebrew name still
remains a bit of a mystery to me. It is 'Yehudah Herzl ben
Eliyohu Fridman'. Now 'Yehudah' comes from my mother's
father, a fascinating man whom I never had the privilege of meeting. He was a Talmud scholar and helped found a very Orthodox
synagogue in London. But he also wrote stories in modern
Hebrew and trained as an artist – something quite scandalous in
its time.

My second name 'Herzl' is not a family name at all. It was
chosen by my father because he was a Zionist and wanted to
honour the name of the founder of that movement, Theodor
Herzl.

I am 'ben Eliyohu', the son of Eliyohu, that is the Hebrew
name 'Elijah'. This was my father's name, and seems to have
been a traditional name in our family. He was 'Eliyohu ben
Menachem Mendel' who was in turn 'Menachem Mendel ben
Eliyohu'.

But where did he get the extra name 'Fridman'? My father was
never able to tell me, beyond the fact that Mr Fridman must have
been a friend of the family whom they wanted to honour in some
way – and how better to honour someone than by naming a child
after them. Perhaps one day I will discover who he was. Meanwhile 'Yehudah Herzl ben Eliyohu' is already as much as most
people can remember when calling me up to the *Torah*, so I tend

to drop 'Fridman'. Perhaps I should be more protective of his memory.

In 'progressive' Jewish circles a new tradition has evolved of adding the name of one's mother as well. Thus my full name would become: Yehudah Herzl ben Eliyohu Fridman v'Esther!

These thoughts were sparked off by a sentence in our *Torah* reading for this *Shabbat*, taken from chapter 17 of the Book of Genesis. When God renews His promise to Abram that he will make him fruitful and the founder of many nations, he also changes his name to Abraham.

> As for Me, behold My covenant is with you, and you shall be the father of a multitude of nations. No longer shall your name be called Avram, but your name shall be Avraham, for a multitude of nations have I given you.

To understand the name change you have to hear a word play in the Hebrew. Avraham will be the *av hamon goyim*, the 'father' (*av*) of *hamon*, a multitude (of *goyim*, 'nations') – though by biblical standards it is not a very good word play.

This change of name is quite familiar in other biblical stories – 'Jacob' becomes 'Israel' and Moses' servant 'Hoshea' becomes 'Joshua'. The only patriarch whose name is not changed is Isaac, because God gave him this name in the first place.

Names in the Hebrew Bible express more than just a way of identifying someone. They also indicate something of the person's character or destiny – so that a change of name is a matter of great importance. When Naomi in the Book of Ruth is embittered about the death of her husband and sons, she demands that people call her instead 'Mara' which means 'bitterness'. Joseph acquires an Egyptian name as a mark of his new status within that society – and in a way he is the first example of a Jew living within two cultures at the same time. Conversely, Queen Esther retains a Hebrew name, Hadassah, which shows her secret loyalty to her people.

There is one occasion still today when traditional Jews may change someone's name. When a child is ill a new additional name is sometimes given him or her, a name they will then use for the rest of their life. It is often a name like 'Raphael' meaning 'God heals' or, for a girl, 'Hayya', meaning 'life'. The tradition is that this extra name will confuse the angel of death so that it will not be able to find the child it is seeking.

So names are markers of different kinds of status – personal, family, social and national. But since we also acquire nicknames or names used by special friends or our family, they come to indicate the different parts that make up our own individual personalities. This is beautifully expressed by the Israeli poet Zelda:

Each person has a name
given him by God
and given him by his father and mother.

Each person has a name
given him by his height and his way of smiling
and given him by his garment.

Each person has a name
given him by the hills
and given him by his walls.

Each person has a name
given him by the stars
and given him by his neighbours.

Each person has a name
given him by his sins
and given him by his longing.

Each person has a name
given him by those who hate him
and given him by his love.

Each person has a name
given him by his festivals
and given him by his work.

Each person has a name
given him by the seasons of the year
and given him by his blindness.

Each person has a name
Given him by the sea
and given him
by his death.

We are made up of so many identities, some forced upon us by others, some we have managed to discover for ourselves; some belong to our own private history, others to the particular collective to which we belong – as people, nation or religion. So do we have a real name, our own inner one by which we know ourselves, the one to which we feel that we must be true? We do not all have the experience of an Abraham – where God pronounces a new name upon us. Sometimes, though, we may experience the struggle of Jacob, emerging from a crisis in our lives with a new sense of who and what we are. More often we may feel like Esther, showing a facade of success and confidence to the outer world, but knowing that we have another private identity within. And sometimes we have to cry out about our inner distress and bitterness like Naomi, and admit that our name no longer fits us. For Naomi, her cry of bitterness and pain became the first step towards her own recovery and a new start in life.

There is a Hasidic story that dramatizes this question about what is the real meaning of our name and shows it in its clearest light. It is told of the Hasidic master Zusya of Hanipol. Shortly before his death he said: 'In the world to come, if they challenge me with the question: "Zusya, Zusya, why were you not like Moses?", then I will be able to answer them – how could I be like

Moses when I am not Moses? But if they ask me: "Zusya, Zusya, why were you not Zusya?" what will I be able to answer them?!'

ANGELS AND ETIQUETTE

(*Vayera* Genesis 18)

In the past month we have experienced the most concentrated period of special days and festivals in the Jewish calendar. The New Year and Day of Atonement have been followed by the Festival of *Sukkot*, Tabernacles, and in turn by *Simchat Torah*, when we complete the weekly cycle of readings from the *Torah* and begin again with Genesis. After the intensity of this period, it is relaxing to turn again to the biblical text, to the stories about the patriarchs, and to try to draw lessons from their daily lives and experiences.

This week's passage from the *Torah, vayera,* begins with chapters eighteen and nineteen of the Book of Genesis and provides us with a mystery and some lessons in etiquette. First the mystery! We are told at the beginning of the chapter that God appears to Abraham while he is sitting in his tent during the hot time of the day. Yet it is not God that Abraham sees but three men. In the conversation that follows it is not sure whether Abraham is speaking to all three of the men, or just one of them, or simply to God. Indeed does Abraham know that he is speaking to God at all? Who are these three mysterious men, or what are they? Is the whole episode simply a figment of Abraham's imagination? After all it is the hottest part of the day. Perhaps they are a mirage, or he is dreaming. Or are they some kind of supernatural beings, sent as messengers by God?

The more we try to understand the passage, and the chapter

that follows, the more our confusion grows. For it seems that one of the 'men' either stays with Abraham or disappears, because in the next chapter there are only two of them. Moreover, in the next chapter they are no longer referred to as 'men' but as 'angels' when they visit Abraham's nephew Lot and rescue him when the towns of Sodom and Gomorrah are destroyed. From the sequence of chapters they would definitely appear to be two of the original three. But if so why are they called something different in the chapter about Abraham from the way they are called in the chapter about Lot?

Firstly we need to clear up a problem in the Hebrew language. The word translated as 'angel' is the Hebrew word *mal'ach*, which actually means 'messenger', someone fulfilling a particular task. When the word was translated for the Greek version of the Bible they chose the Greek word for 'messenger', angelos, from which comes our word 'angel'. It is only later traditions that turned these 'messengers' into the supernatural 'angels' that we think of today with wings and feathers.

So on one level of the story, it is three men who encounter Abraham bringing him a message from God. Two of them will then continue their journey to Sodom and Gomorrah to rescue Lot.

The rabbis were a bit critical about Lot, and in this they were following the biblical evaluation of him. His wealth is all derived from Abraham, but that very wealth leads to the two men quarreling and separating. Lot, it seems, was a bit too much concerned with his financial situation which made him forget certain other values about family loyalty and respect. This leads to the rabbinic explanation of why the mysterious visitors are sometimes called 'men' and sometimes 'angels'. Although Abraham only saw 'men' approaching him, strangers, probably idol worshippers, he was such a generous host that he went out into the heat of the day to greet them and showed them great hospitality. But Lot, on the other hand, was so mean that if he had only seen two men coming he would have ignored them. However because they appeared to him looking like 'angels', supernatural beings, he was willing to greet them and look after them!

Rabbinic tradition develops the story a bit further and identifies the angels. The rabbis pointed out that this story occurs just after Abraham has circumcised himself and his first son Ishmael. Since this was a major operation, no wonder Abraham was lying down in his tent recovering from the trauma. So the first messenger was Raphael, the angel appointed to look after the process of healing. He was there to help Abraham recover. The second was the angel Michael whose task was to give Abraham's wife Sarah the good news that she would have a child. The third was Gabriel whose task was to destroy the wicked cities of Sodom and Gomorrah.

The rabbis derived a number of important lessons from these stories about how we should behave. From Abraham's actions they taught the importance of hospitality, for Abraham went out of his way to look for, welcome and feed his guests. In the same way we should also be generous hosts.

From God's behaviour we learn the *mitzvah*, the commandment, of *bikkur cholim*, visiting the sick. We too should imitate the actions of God and visit those who are ill and support and comfort them.

The rabbis also noticed a difference between the behaviour of the visitors in the two chapters. When Abraham offered them food they ate it at once. When Lot offered them hospitality at first they refused and only accepted when he insisted. From this they derived the responsibility of guests. Abraham was clearly a rich man and could afford to feed them, so they did not refuse. But it was not clear whether Lot was wealthy and could afford to be so generous, so they refused hospitality at first so as not to embarrass him. Only when he insisted did they agree.

If these are the lessons in etiquette to be derived from the chapter we are left with the mystery of these visitors and how to understand them. One approach is to see them as normal human beings who happen to be messengers for someone else even if they are unaware of it themselves. This means that any encounter with another person contains a message for us, some kind of spiritual lesson, for everyone is made in the image of God. If we behave like Lot we will never learn this, or recognize the message when it comes to us, because we will always be looking for the extraordinary, for the supernatural, for angels with wings and feathers. But if we are like Abraham, then we will treat each person we meet as a potential guest and will listen out for the special message they have for us, the message that only we can hear, the message that is meant for us alone.

LIKE ONE WHO SINGS LOVE SONGS

(*Vayera* Genesis 18–22)

Our *parashah*, *Vayera*, covers a number of significant events and journeys in the life of Abraham. In reading through the chapters we become particularly aware of the nomadic nature of Abraham's life. We begin at a place called the 'terebinths of Mamre' where he receives three visitors with special news about his future. In the next episode he journeys towards the Negev and finds pasture and water in a place called Gerar. At the end of our section he settles in Beersheva. Abraham was on a journey, both physical and spiritual, throughout his life. The only permanent home he found in the land promised to him by God was his grave in Hebron.

It seemed to me that this was an appropriate image for this week as we begin to think about the event sixty years ago in Germany known as Kristallnacht, the 'night of broken glass', 9th November 1938. In that one night synagogues throughout Germany were burned, Jewish shops were destroyed and Jews were attacked in the streets. It marked the climax of a process of intimidation and destruction of Jewish life in Germany which had already led many to take their own road into exile. They too followed the path trod millennia before by Abraham and so many individual Jews and Jewish communities in the intervening centuries.

For this *Shabbat* I do not want to focus on a biblical text but on other texts, ones not usually associated with Jewish tradition. In fact they belong to a genre of writing that is rarely considered of any particular consequence in Jewish life, though it is an important element of the Jewish culture of this century. The texts belong to songs, the popular songs and cabaret songs of the twenties, especially in Berlin, some of which were the products of assimilated Jews who played a major role in German politics, culture and art. One particular song of that era has had a renewed lease of life in Germany in recent years because of the popularity of one group of singers – the Comedian Harmonists. The group was massively popular in the twenties and early thirties, both in Germany and internationally, and received the kind of adulation we know from the Beatles.

Their story has become well known because of a television documentary about them, the re-release of their records and a major feature film and stage productions reviving their close harmony style of singing and humour. The founder of the group and two of the other performers were Jewish, the other three were not, and the group was forced to split under the Nazi laws governing public performances which forbade 'Aryans' to perform with 'non-Aryans'. The three Jews were fortunate in finding a new home in America, one of them eventually having a long and successful career as a Cantor in a synagogue.

One of their most popular songs was written by Robert Gilbert and composed by Werner Richard Heymann, both of them of Jewish origin. It has a haunting, sentimental melody. The song first appeared in a German musical film in 1932, 'Ein blonder Traum'. Within a year the author and composer had gone into exile in America. So a simple entertainment song takes on an almost prophetic significance.

Somewhere out in the world there's a little bit of luck
and I dream of it each moment of my life.

Somewhere out in the world there's a bit of happiness
and I've dreamt of it for such a long, long time.
If I knew where it was I would search the world for this.
In my heart, just for once, how I'd like to know such bliss.
Somewhere out in the world there's a heaven to be won,
just somewhere, just somehow, just somewhen.[1]

It is not alone in echoing a yearning for another better place.
The composer Friedrich Schwarz, also of Jewish origin, was
politically engaged in the struggle against the Nazi party as it rose
to power, attacking them with his pamphlets. Under constant
threat he too was forced to leave Germany. In 1933 he wrote a
song on the eve of his departure. Its title was 'Ich hab' kein
Heimatland', 'I have no homeland', but his own name for it was
a 'jüdische Tango', 'a Jewish tango'. It was eventually recorded by
the orchestra of Marek Weber and sung by John Hendrik. This
did not take place in Germany but in London where the performers too had been forced to emigrate. In July 1933 Friedrich
Schwartz was found dead in his hotel room in Paris. The evidence, that was never properly investigated, suggested that he
had been murdered.

With these Jewish composers and lyricists, and the many
others who left, went their songs, for they too were banned.

Two Biblical passages offer ironic comments on the fate of
these Jewish songwriters and their songs. One is Psalm 137, a song
full of the anger and bitterness of a people forced into exile. It is
the prototype of all partisan songs of resistance. This time the

---

[1] Irgendwo auf der Welt gibt's ein kleines bisschen Glück
und ich träum davon in jedem Augenblick.
Irgendwo auf der Welt gibt's ein bisschen Seligkeit,
und ich träum davon schon lange, lange Zeit.
Wenn ich wüsst wo das ist, ging ich in die Welt hinein,
denn ich möcht einmal recht so von Herzen glücklich sein.
Irgendwo auf der Welt fängt der Weg zum Himmel an.
Irgendwo, irgendwie, irgendwann!

enemy, the Babylonian conquerors, *did* want to hear Jewish
songs, the songs of the Jerusalem Temple they had destroyed,
perhaps to taunt their captives with the fact that their God, too,
was defeated. But the Levites, the musicians who had sung in the
Temple, refused:

> By the rivers of Babylon
> there we sat down
> there too we wept
> when we remembered Zion.
> On the willows there,
> we hung up our harps,
> for there our captors asked of us songs,
> our oppressors for joyful ones:
> Sing us the songs of Zion.
> How can we sing the song of the Eternal
> on foreign soil?

Instead of the songs of the Temple the writer invokes a curse
upon himself: let the hand with which he plays his instrument
and the tongue with which he sings, become useless if he should
forget Jerusalem.

The other passage is different. It is the complaint of the
prophet Ezekiel, who couched his words of warning in the form
of songs, only to find them ignored, treated as if they were merely
entertainment and of no significance.

> And lo you are to them like one who sings love songs with a
> beautiful voice and plays well on an instrument, for they hear
> what you say, but will not do it. When this comes, and come it
> will, then they will know that a prophet has been among them.
> (Ezekiel 33.32–33)

I would not want to suggest that the popular songs by the
Jewish composers of pre-war Germany were prophetic texts to
be studied with intensity and added to the biblical canon. But
they are another facet of that extraordinary Jewish creativity and

artistry that could be found there and was all but destroyed and lost. This too we should remember on Kristallnacht.

Once again Robert Gilbert and Werner Richard Heymann say it for us in their song from the 1932 film, 'Der Kongress tanzt'.

> This comes just one time,
> and never more times
> for it is far too beautiful to last …
> This comes just one time
> and never more times
> perhaps it only is a daydream that is past!
> Though life might give it
> for just a minute,
> by tomorrow it has surely passed
> and what has passed us is forever past.[1]

---

[1] Das gibt's nur einmal,
das kommt nicht wieder,
das ist zu schön, um wahr zu sein …
Das gibt's nur einmal,
das kommt nicht wieder,
das ist vielleicht nur Träumerei!
Das kann das Leben
nur einmal geben,
vielleicht ist's morgen schon vorbei!
und was vorbei ist, ist vorbei!

DEATH AND TAXES

(*Chayei Sara* Genesis 23.1–25.18)

There are two themes that run through our *Torah* reading for this *Shabbat*. Last week we read the story of the binding of Isaac (Genesis 22), one of the most dramatic highpoints of the whole *Torah*. Will Abraham sacrifice his son? Why does God make such a cruel demand? Will Isaac survive – and if he dies, what will happen to God's promise that Abraham's seed would inherit the land? But now, after all this high drama, come two scenes of simple domestic matters. In Genesis 23 we are told that Sarah, Abraham's wife, dies and Abraham sets out on the complex set of negotiations to secure her a place of burial. Then in chapter 24 he sends his servant to seek out a wife for his son Isaac.

At one level these two events reflect the working out of certain major themes of the Book of Genesis. God has promised to Abraham and his seed the entire land of Israel and we see here the first step towards the fulfilment of this promise – though it is ironic that the only part of the promised land that Abraham actually comes to own is this place in which he will one day be buried. In a similar way the quest for a wife for his son Isaac has importance for the future. Without a wife there will be no next generation and the dream of a nation to come from his descendants will also fail. In fact in these two stories we see the personal outcome within Abraham's lifetime of the promise given to him by God at the start of his spiritual journey – 'Go from your land, your birthplace and the house of your father to the land that I will show you and I will make you into a great nation' (Genesis 12.1–2). The beginnings of the fulfilment of the promise, owner-ship of the land and a great future nation, are present in these closing events in the life of the father of the Jewish people, *Avraham Avinu,* 'Abraham, our father'.

But while both these chapters point to far-reaching conse-quences, there is also a simpler level on which they can be under-stood.

It was in Vienna that I first heard a description of the two essential factors of human life, from the landlady at the Pension where I was staying. I had been speaking to her about how busy I was, how I must do this and I must do that! She added, 'and you must pay taxes and you must die!' Death and taxes – the two inevitable features of life.

These two stories about Abraham are not about taxes – though he seems to have had to pay quite a lot extra money in order to purchase the cave in Machpelah. But they are certainly about death, the awareness of our own death and the need to prepare for it in the right way. Perhaps it was the death of Sarah that made Abraham take steps to ensure the future of his family by seeking a wife for Isaac. With the death of Sarah came the real-ization of his own mortality. We have to bury our dead and we have to prepare the way, as far as we are able, for the generation that will come after us. Abraham sets about doing both of these duties.

But what is surprising is the amount of space the Bible devotes to these two activities, especially the latter. With sixty-seven verses to it, the story of the finding of a wife for Isaac is one of the longest chapters in the whole of the Bible. The journey of Abraham's servant, his choosing of Rebeccah as he stands by the well, the long negotiations with her family and the journey back home, could all have been described in a couple of sentences. In fact many events or episodes that would seem to be of far greater significance in the Bible are described in a very brief way.

This puzzle was already noted by the rabbis in the Midrash. Rabbi Acha compares the length of the chapter with the brevity of some of the commandments that appear later, and comments: 'The table talk of the servants of the households of the Patriarchs is more beautiful than the *Torah* of their descendants' (Genesis Rabbah 60.11). So scholars in every generation have studied every detail of the negotiations between the servant and Laban's family to understand his strategy and also to find guidelines for our own correct behaviour.

But what interests me today is not the details of such matters but the space devoted to them. It is not only the heroic moments in the lives of the Patriarchs that are recorded and preserved – like the challenge of the *Akeda*, 'the binding of Isaac', or Abraham's military prowess when he rescues his nephew Lot, or Isaac's struggle to preserve the wells dug by his father. The Bible is also deeply concerned with these domestic moments, the familiar things that are part of our own everyday life: coming to terms with the death of those we love and doing our duty by them; planning and working for the future of our children. It is in these private events we take so much for granted that the religious truths of our own lives are to be discovered.

This emphasis is picked up by the rabbis as well. They teach that *ma'aseh avot siman l'vanim*, 'the deeds of the fathers are signs for the children': we are to read the stories of the patriarchs and see in their behaviour models for what we also should do. But what are the models the rabbis emphasize? We are not told to imitate Abraham in the case of the *Akeda*, to offer up our own sons – that was seen as a once-only event, never to be repeated. Instead they tell stories about Abraham's hospitality, how he went out of his way to greet strangers, welcome them to his tent and feed them. That is how we are to behave. They also taught that Abraham and Sarah used to encourage people to come under the wings of God and convert to Judaism. It is Abraham as the model of a good family man, generous to others and religiously welcoming, that they tried to portray and ask us to imitate.

It is in the way we conduct ourselves in the details of our life, how we treat family and friends, those we work with and those who work for us; the care with which we fulfil our duties, to the the dead as well as to the living; the way we respond to those in need; the responsibility we take for those we love and the way we try to become reconciled to those with whom we are in conflict; our willingness to recognize our faults and failures and seek to correct them – it is in these everyday realities that we are to look for the religious truth of our lives.

For we alone write the chapters of our life, the long and the short ones, as we would like them to be. As the chasidim taught: we should so lead our lives that every event, like those of the patriarchs, can become scripture.

DEMONIZING THE OTHER

(*Vayishlach* Obadiah)

Today's *Haftarah*, the reading from the prophets, consists of the entire book of Obadiah. And it makes very depressing reading because it seems to stand in complete contrast to the passage from the *Torah* that it accompanies. In Genesis 33 and 34 we read of the meeting between Jacob and Esau after twenty years of separation. Jacob approaches the meeting very cautious and afraid – because Esau is coming out to greet him with a large number of men. And Jacob has good reason to be worried about his brother, having stolen his blessing from him all those years ago. But when they actually meet, Esau embraces and kisses Jacob and it seems that there has been a complete reconciliation. Nevertheless there are clearly some anxieties left in Jacob, or perhaps he is also quite realistic about Esau's residual anger. When Esau offers to travel with him, or at least leave a number of men to accompany him, Jacob finds excuses to keep the two groups separate. Having met and created an uneasy peace between them, it is better not to risk further conflict. As the Yiddish proverb has it, *A shlechter sholem iz besser vi a guter krig.* – 'A bad peace is better than a good war.'

In surprising contrast to this mood of reconciliation, the Book of Obadiah is a fierce attack on the kingdom of Edom, a country to the south east of Palestine, where the descendants of Esau lived. Obadiah refers to a time when the Edomites took advantage of Israel's destruction to invade and loot and kill the survivors. Instead of the reconciliation described in Genesis, the book of Obadiah points to a long-standing state of conflict between the descendants of the two brothers. The prophet predicts the downfall of Edom, when they shall themselves be treated as they treated their brother Jacob. In the end, Israel shall be restored to its territories and will rule the mountain of Esau, and God's rule will be established over the whole region.

The Jacob and Esau stories, and the other biblical passages that refer to Edom, reflect real political issues of that period. Obadiah's feeling of betrayal has its historical origins in Edom's attack on Jerusalem after it fell to the Babylonians but his feelings are heightened because Edom or Esau was Jacob's brother. For a brother to act in such a way is doubly shameful.

But if Obadiah's anger at Edom is understandable in his own time, why did the rabbis centuries later choose it as the Haftarah for this particular passage from the *Torah*? Surely the reconciliation of Jacob and Esau was something to be welcomed and it could have been emphasized in the *Haftarah* as well. Why point instead to the negative aspects?

Part of the answer lies in the biblical texts about Edom. Instead of just being a particular nation Edom seems to symbolize all the destructive political powers that seek to blot out the memory of Israel and Israel's God. This led the rabbis in later centuries to identify Edom as the great Roman empire that had conquered Palestine.

Because of the dangers they faced under occupation, the rabbis had to disguise their criticism of the Roman authorities and speak in a veiled way about them. So the name Edom became their code word for the Romans, and they were able to retell the stories of Jacob and Esau to bring out a message for their own time. In the Bible itself Esau is very much the wronged brother; he seems to be rather simple and certainly not wicked; and, judging by his behaviour when Jacob returned, quite a generous and loving person. Yet the rabbis turned his character inside out and made him a great villain with murderous intentions against Jacob, because they could use the stories about him to talk about the crimes of Rome.

So it may be that when the rabbis chose Obadiah for the *Haftarah*, it was a comment upon their current situation of oppression by Rome – and their hope, that just as in his prophecy, this oppression would end and Israel would be restored to its land and proper position.

The biblical texts about Edom could still serve today for describing any power that sought to destroy either the Jewish people or their religious message. Yet it is precisely here that we come into very dangerous waters. Broadcasting in Germany makes it rather difficult to say the following, but clearly from a Jewish point of view the whole Nazi regime was a modern Edom, the arrogant kingdom, reborn into the world. Moreover the words of Obadiah exactly describe the behaviour of those who collaborated in the destruction of the Jewish people:

> You should not have gloated
> over the day of your brother
> in the day of his misfortune;
> you should not have rejoiced over the people of Judah
> in the day of their ruin;
> you should not have boasted in the day of distress.
> You should not have entered the gate of my people
> in the day of his calamity;
> you should not have gloated over his disaster
> in the day of his calamity;
> you should not have looted his goods
> in the day of calamity.
> You should not have stood at the parting of the ways
> to cut off his fugitives;
> you should not have delivered up his survivors
> in the day of distress. (Obadiah 12–14)

Through the language of the prophet we can hear the sense of betrayal and shock, the pain and the horror at seeing a world he thought he trusted turning on him to destroy him.

Yet precisely the power of this passage is itself a problem. Because having such potent images can lead us to identify any opponent as a new Edom. And the risk is that by using that symbolic language and reviving these old fears and memories, we distort our perception of today's reality, and even prevent ourselves seeing the humanity, and the particularity, of the other. It is difficult enough to resolve conflicts, especially when there has been a breakdown of communication, and violence has replaced talking and reasoning together. But if we allow or encourage the old mythological images of the past to colour our thinking about the other, it becomes doubly difficult to return to any possibility of meeting.

The Gulf War allowed all sides to borrow from their stock of ancient demons so as to characterize the other. Every nationalist conflict throughout the world thrives on memories of ancient enmities, of past defeats and insults, old betrayals and victories, so as to justify current excesses and violence. We all have our Edoms to remember and use to demonize our enemies.

So to read the prophet Obadiah today is depressing. Surely there is enough hatred in the world without justifying it with old religious memories.

But perhaps we can read into the rabbinic choice of this passage a warning about what can go wrong if we do not work at reconciliation. Perhaps it is not inevitable that Esau the brother will turn into Edom the murderer. Jacob and Esau continued to live apart – maybe they were never prepared to risk the next step of building trust and understanding. For all neighbouring peoples who are in conflict, the hardest human task is to find the right balance between maintaining their distinct identity and sharing the world with others. But however painful it may be to attempt to overcome our own prejudices and fears and try to build real trust between peoples, the alternative is the violence and endless residual hatred that Obadiah reflects. So it is better to work and pray for the promise offered by our *Torah* reading, when the brothers finally meet:

> Then Esau ran to meet Jacob and he hugged him and fell upon his neck and kissed him, and both of them wept. (Genesis 33.4)

FROM ABRAHAM TO ISAAC

(*Toledot* Genesis 25.19–28.9)

This week's *parashah* from the Book of Genesis introduces a crucial turning point in Jewish history. Abraham has been chosen by God to found a new people with a particular religious faith and commitment. We have read about Abraham's experiences during the latter part of his life, events that the rabbis designated as ten tests designed to refine him even further and at the same time to display his qualities to the outside world. Now Abraham is dead, buried by his two sons Isaac and Ishmael. But what will happen to his vision, his experience of God, the promises and blessings God gave to him? Will Isaac be able to follow in the footsteps of his father or will the great adventure stop with this change of generation?

The *parashah* begins with a strangely repetitious sentence: 'And these are the generations of Isaac son of Abraham; Abraham begat Isaac' (Genesis 25.19). If Isaac is the son of Abraham, why repeat the idea with different words: 'Abraham begat Isaac'? One obvious answer is that this is simply biblical style – the repetition emphasizing the fact and indeed the important point that Abraham does have in Isaac a true successor. So we could understand it to mean that Isaac was not only Abraham's physical son, but also his spiritual son, heir to the blessing and the task of witnessing to God in the world.

For some reason the rabbis took a different, and somewhat bizarre, line. The great mediaeval commentator Rashi quotes from the Midrash.

Since scripture wrote, 'Isaac, son of Abraham', it felt compelled to add the words 'Abraham begat Isaac' because the cynics of those days used to say that Sarah became pregnant through King Avimelech, the king who thought Sarah was Abraham's sister and took her into his harem. Why did they think this? Because Sarah had lived so many years with Abraham without becoming pregnant! Now, just after her time with Avimelech, she was about to have a baby! So what did God do? He shaped Isaac's face so that it looked exactly like Abraham, so that everyone knew that Abraham was the father of Isaac. (Midrash Tanchuma)

Abraham Ibn Ezra, the other great mediaeval Bible commentator from Spain, tends to prefer more rational explanations for unusual expressions in the Bible. Nevertheless he quotes this rabbinic view before adding another explanation that the verb 'begat' can also mean to raise a child, which he suggests is the real explanation here.

Even Rashi's explanation can be understood in other than simply sexual terms. The question of who is the real child of Abraham, or who is the real father of Isaac, is about what ideas and influences are handed down from one generation to the next. The rabbis in their time were struggling to establish Judaism on the basis of new ideas, and they turned to the stories of the patriarchs for support. But since the changes they were making were quite radical, perhaps they needed to insist that they were simply continuing an unbroken tradition, Isaac was really identical with Abraham. Rashi, living in Christian France and Germany at the time of the crusades, was trying to ensure that the Jewish community remained loyal to the faith of their ancestors, despite the trauma of their times. So it would have been important to stress the idea that Abraham's teaching had been faithfully handed down to the next generation. Both periods could use the story for their own legitimate purposes.

But here we encounter a major tension in Jewish thought. According to another midrash not only did Isaac's face look exactly like Abraham his father but this happened from his very birth – and he even had a beard like Abraham! In this version the child, the next generation, is exactly identical with the generation that has gone before. Contrast this with another rabbinic view. The rabbis ask the question why the Amidah prayer, the central prayer in every Jewish service, does not simply say, 'God of Abraham, Isaac and Jacob'. Instead it is very explicit: *God* of Abraham, *God* of Isaac and *God* of Jacob. Why this emphatic repetition of the word 'God'? Because each generation of the patriarchs experienced God in different ways and had to discover God for themselves. By this reading, the new generation is *not* identical with the previous one. So how reconcile these two contradictory views? The rabbis draw our attention to the opening words of the prayer: 'Blessed are You, Eternal, *our* God and God of our *fathers*'. There is both continuity and discontinuity between the generations. We may each of us experience God in a new way, but nevertheless we attach ourselves to the experience of God of those who have gone before. Nothing is exactly the same but nothing is entirely new.

The Jewish world today can be divided into two camps among those who follow a religious path. Some emphasize that they are really identical with Abraham, that their faith and practice is exactly the same as that of previous generations and that they feel a responsibility to preserve things unchanged into the future. What they sometimes fail to recognize is that Abraham was himself a rebel against the religious ideas of his own father – he had to leave home to found a new kind of faith in God. However, others see themselves as Isaac, inheritors of the tradition of Abraham, but concerned to discover God and the way to serve God out of their own experience of the world. What they sometimes forget is how faithful Isaac was in preserving the work of his father – symbolized by his reinstating of the wells dug by

Abraham that had been filled in or stolen. What is tragic for the Jewish world is that both groups tend to view their positions in absolute terms: the Abrahams condemn the Isaacs for the changes they have made, and the Isaacs condemn the Abrahams for not recognizing that the world has moved on and that new dimensions of Judaism are needed.

Both views are important, of course, for the health of Judaism and the Jewish people, and indeed of any religious community, though a little more tolerance between the different groups would be welcome. We need both the preservers of the past and the shapers of the future, for within the tension they create we live out our Jewish existence today.

JACOB OR ISRAEL?

(*Vayetzei* Genesis 28.10–32.3)

The biblical patriarch Jacob is an extraordinary character. Two of the most famous images to be found in the Bible belong to his personal story.

One of them is Jacob's midnight struggle with the mysterious man or angel. It led to his name being changed from Jacob to Israel, though the struggle left him limping.

But the other image comes from our reading this *Shabbat*. Jacob has stolen the blessing that belonged to his brother Esau. Now, in fear of his life, he has to leave home on his way into exile. He cannot know at this moment that it will be twenty years before he returns to his homeland, years of suffering but also years of great material success. Since the blessing he stole was all about material success that is not surprising, but Jacob cannot have realized at the time what a price in pain he would have to pay.

But all that is ahead of him. Now he is simply alone. Later he will speak of this moment and remember that all he took with him from home when he crossed the Jordan river was his shepherd's staff. He arrives at a place where he will stay the night. Jacob falls asleep and dreams the famous dream of the ladder reaching up to heaven, the other great biblical image that comes from his life.

> And he dreamed and behold! there was a ladder set up on the earth, and the top of it reached to heaven; and behold! the

angels of God were ascending and descending on it! And
behold! the Eternal stood above it ... (Genesis 28.12–13)

The rabbis were puzzled by one aspect of this dream. If angels
are heavenly beings then surely they should be coming down the
ladder from heaven and only then going up it. But the biblical
text specifically puts it the other way round. First they are
described as going from the ground upwards towards heaven
and only then coming down. The rabbis found one explanation
that fits very closely to Jacob's personal situation at this time.

In this interpretation, these figures on the ladder were the
guardian angels that protected Jacob. But the ones that had been
looking after him throughout his life till now were restricted to
the land of Israel. Now that he was about to leave the land, their
task was completed and they were returning to their base; other
angels would now take over to protect him on the journey to
other places. Jacob had fallen asleep at the border post at the edge
of the land of Israel.

In his dream Jacob does not try to climb the ladder himself. He
remains earthbound. Even when God speaks to him Jacob fails to
understand the full implications of what is said.

> I am the Eternal, the God of Abraham your father and the
> God of Isaac. The land on which you lie I will give to you and
> to your descendants; and your descendants shall be like the
> dust of the earth, and you shall spread abroad to the west and
> to the east and to the north and to the south. And by you and
> your descendants shall all the families of the earth be blessed.
> Behold, I am with you and will keep you wherever you go, and
> will bring you back to this land, for I will not leave you till I
> have done that of which I have spoken to you. (vv. 13–15)

God spells out the entire vision of Abraham's blessing and the
destiny of the Jewish people; to spread throughout the world but
also to live in this special land; to become a blessing for all the

peoples of the earth. It is a dazzling and challenging destiny. But Jacob is not ready yet to comprehend what he has heard. His personal situation is too frightening and his immediate needs too great – they overwhelm any long-term ambitions he might have. So when he responds he makes no mention at all of the promise of Abraham. Instead he offers a vow of his own to God, but one that only speaks about his personal needs:

> If God will be with me, and will keep in in this way that I go, and will give me bread to eat and clothing to wear, so that I come again to my father's house in peace, then the Eternal shall be my God, and this stone which I have set up for a pillar, shall be God's house; and of all that You give me I will give the tenth to you. (vv. 20–22)

'Just get me home safely', he asks, 'with food to eat and clothing on my back – that is my only ambition at this moment.' It is partly a promise to God, partly a kind of bargain. Jacob is still Jacob and not yet Israel. Till now all that we know of him is that he is tricky and willing to be dishonest. He seems to be the least likely person for God to want to choose to carry on Abraham's task of bringing blessing to all the peoples of the world. But this same Jacob can also dream dreams, can have a vision of a ladder rising to heaven. So there is also within him the promise of a greater quality to his life that could emerge. He could become two quite different people: the Jacob who steals and cheats or the Israel who wrestles with God and on behalf of God. That is why his name keeps changing back and forth in the different stories about him – Jacob becomes Israel, Israel becomes Jacob.

Before his spiritual self can fully emerge, all of his trickiness and practicality will also be tested. Ahead lies the meeting with Laban his future father-in-law who is more than a match for Jacob when it comes to being tricky and dishonest. Jacob will see in Laban, as if in a distorting mirror, all of the worst of his own qualities. That must make him reconsider his own actions. But he will also meet angels on other occasions in his life, and with one he will struggle all night. But is Jacob trying to pin the angel to the ground, to bring him down to his own level; or is he trying to force his way up the ladder to heaven and overcome the angel who stands in his way? These two key pictures from Jacob's life, the ladder and the struggle, actually belong together.

Today we meet fewer angels, or if we meet them we do not recognize them for what they are. But we can understand the struggle, for we each contain within us a Jacob and an Israel, the material and the spiritual, the earthbound and the heavenly, the part of us that manipulates other people and the part of us that has the potential to bring a blessing to the whole world. And just as Jacob keeps changing to Israel and back again, so the struggle within us is never over till the day we die.

BROTHERLY LOVE

(*Vayishlach* Genesis 32.4–36.43)

The story in this week's *Torah* portion is one of the most dramatic in the Bible. Jacob is on his way home and about to confront his twin brother Esau. As in so many other stories about brothers in the Hebrew Bible, there is a history of conflict between them. Jacob had stolen the blessing that was due to his brother, and now, twenty years later, he was afraid of Esau's reaction when he came back. Did Esau still hate him? How would he react when they met?

The first two brothers in the Hebrew Bible are Cain and Abel. When Cain was jealous of his brother Abel, he killed him. As we read about Jacob we have in the back of our minds the Cain and Abel story. Is violence the only possible result when brothers are in conflict?

But surely brothers should love and support each other? Today we talk about 'brotherly love' and 'brotherliness' as if we could assume that these are positive things that we can take for granted. Yet all too often brothers, and sisters too, have a deep-seated rivalry, competing from childhood for the attention or favour or love of their parents. The family situation is the microcosm of the world. It is the framework in which we learn to orientate ourselves. So the relationships we establish in our childhood will colour our expectations and behaviour in later life. Being brothers ties us together with biological bonds, so there are great expectations about how we should support and love each other. But if that love or affection are not there, the

closeness merely exacerbates the jealousies and anger that may
also be present. The love between brothers cannot simply be
assumed or taken for granted. Instead it may be the hardest love
of all to establish. Because we are bound together by blood, we
have an even greater responsibility to build some kind of proper
relationship. Real brotherly love is not just a sentimental matter,
it has to be earned. Yet if it can be achieved it can help transform
the world.

We read the story about Jacob's return to meet his brother
Esau in Genesis chapter 32 and 33, and see the events through the
eyes of Jacob alone. When he sends messengers to greet Esau we
learn nothing about what Esau thinks or feels. The messengers
simply report back to Jacob that Esau is on his way with a retinue
of four hundred men. Jacob has to guess what this means – a
parade of people coming to honour him or an army coming
to destroy him. Like Jacob we also do not know, so we can only
follow his response, equally uncertain of the outcome.

The rabbis believed that the biblical stories were intended to
give us models for our own behaviour, so they paid close attention to what Jacob did. Since they had the same experience of
confronting a hostile and threatening world, they looked to
Jacob's actions for some guidance or strategy for the survival of
the Jewish people.

They saw in Jacob's actions a preparation for three eventuali-
ties. They described them with three words: gifts, prayer and
battle. He sent a gift ahead of him to his brother in an attempt to
appease him and fend off his anger. He prayed to God for help
and support at this time. He prepared to fight by dividing up his
encampment so that at least half of them would survive if he was
defeated.

The first of Jacob's actions can be understood in both a
positive and a negative way. When we are faced by a potential
conflict it is essential to attempt to open up a dialogue. Violence
is the result of the failure of human reason, common sense and

generosity of spirit to come up with some sort of solution. But someone has to be the first to make the gesture of appeasement that makes negotiation possible. The problem is that we often fear that such a gesture will only lead to further demands that we cannot accept. Moreover in this century the word 'appeasement' has come to be associated with a simple surrender. All too often those who are the aggressors have seen the desire to negotiate a solution as a sign of weakness that can be exploited further. Yet the attempt to seek reconciliation is actually proof not of weakness but of true inner strength and moral power. Human life is more important than personal pride. So Jacob's first ploy is to try to avert violence.

He tries a human action before he turns to God for help. This is also the sign of a person with religious faith. In the end what happens is in the hands of God, but we must not set aside our own human responsibility and leave it entirely to God. Our intelligence and strength and moral values are tools that have been given to us by God, so it is for us to use them as best we can. We ourselves are the agents through whom God acts. There is a delightful Jewish story that illustrates this.

There has been a flood and everyone has evacuated the small town, everyone except one elderly pious Jew. When the car came to collect him and take him away to safety he said: 'I will stay here because I have faith in God and I know that He will save me.' The floodwaters came and he had to move upstairs. A rowing boat came by to take him to safety through the window, but again he refused, insisting that he had prayed to God and knew that God would protect him. The waters rose higher and he had to climb on the roof. A helicopter came by and the pilot called to him to climb aboard and be taken away. Again he refused: he had faith that God would save him whatever happened. The waters rose higher, and he drowned! When he got to the gates of heaven, he was extremely angry and shouted, 'I have dedicated my life to serving You, God, and I had faith that you would save me, how

could you let me down in this way?' To which God replied: 'I
don't understand what happened, I sent a car, a rowing boat and
a helicopter to fetch you!'

Jacob's third action is to prepare for battle. Resistance and a
fight may be the final desperate action that we have to take.
Violence is the last resort, not the first.

Prayer to God for help stands between the attempt at reconciliation and the final resort of physical resistance and violence.
Our human responsibility is not removed – instead it is emphasized as the major task we must set ourselves when confronting a
conflict situation. This also means that to use religion to justify
violence against others is a *chillul hashem*, a desecration of God's
name and a travesty of religious values. Faith in God begins with
faith in the possibility of human reconciliation and mutual
respect.

Jacob and Esau are brothers in conflict with each other. The
image of Cain and Abel stands before them. Can they break this
pattern of human conflict and violence? How they behave to
each other will create a model for generations to come.

> Then Esau ran to greet Jacob, and embraced him, and fell
> upon his shoulder and kissed him and both of them wept.
> (Genesis 33.4)

Whenever brothers long separated from each other meet, the
same tensions may be present. Germany has seen the reuniting of
brothers and sisters and experienced both the joy and the painful
reality of misunderstanding, envy, fear and anger. Germany
is experiencing today the presence of other human brothers
and sisters – different only in nationality and faith. The same
choices are present today as they were when Cain killed Abel or
Jacob and Esau were reconciled. If Jacob and Esau do not meet
and embrace, then Cain will stalk the land. We can become
murderers and accomplices to murder, or we can become those
who try to welcome our brothers and sisters, to understand

them, to respect their differences, to value their qualities, and to find a way of living together in peace.

When Jacob finally meets Esau having completed all his preparations, Esau does the exact opposite of what Jacob has expected. Instead of enmity he embraces him, instead of a weapon, he brings him a kiss. Jacob's courage meets Esau's generosity. The true qualities of brotherhood appear. And the violence that seemed inevitable never happens.

That, of course, is not the end of the story, but only the beginning. Too much history stands between them for their differences and mistrust to disappear overnight. They will need to keep a certain distance from each other and to respect the differences between them. They will need to build on this moment of reconciliation to ensure that it works in the future, for themselves and for their children after them. They will have to create agreements to ensure their mutual protection and make commitments to enforce them. They will need regular opportunities to meet, formal discussions to resolve differences, ritualised ceremonies to build trust and confidence between them, but also family gatherings where personal bonds can be established. They will need to take mutual responsibility for each other and act effectively against those who seek to stir up hatred between them. Brotherhood is not built by slogans or good will alone. But the alternative to that hard work is violence and a destructiveness that harms all sides.

In today's pluralistic society in Europe, we live together as brothers and sisters, each taking responsibility for each other, or else we die together as strangers and enemies. We can be Cain and Abel or we can be Jacob and Esau – the choice is ours.

> Then Esau ran to greet Jacob, and embraced him, and fell upon his shoulder and kissed him and both of them wept. (Genesis 33.4)

WINTER

THE JOURNEY TO ONESELF

(*Shemot* Exodus 1.1–6.1)

At the heart of Jewish tradition and values is a dissatisfaction with the world as it presently is. Ours is a very activist religion, constantly pushing towards some kind of improvement – in ourselves and in the world around us. We are in that sense a driven people, aware that before us lie certain messianic hopes for the betterment of all of humanity. One way of expressing this belief that the world is still on a journey to healing and perfection is through the contrasting images of slavery and freedom. The starting point for these images is the biblical book, *Shemot*, Exodus, which we begin to read this *Shabbat*. Unless we understand the degradation of slavery, we cannot understand or fully value the ideal of freedom, so it becomes an essential part of our tradition to re-enact the transition from one to the other. Through reading the stories of the Exodus and through the various elements of the Festival of Passover, we re-experience that journey from slavery to freedom, and become each time reborn into a new awareness of the meaning and value of life.

Our whole religious calendar is built upon a recurrent cycle that starts with the Exodus from Egypt as the point of our liberation, when we became defined as a distinct and unique people. We encounter God at Sinai at the festival of *Shavuot*, Pentecost, and re-experience the wandering in the wilderness at *Sukkot*, Tabernacles. But then the cycle begins again from the start and we become slaves once again, yearning to be free.

But this cycle says something about our nature as the Jewish people. We are restless wanderers, never content with the status quo, always aware of how easy it is to slide into some sort of complacency about the way things are. Nor is our quest for a newer, better world a purely internal or selfish matter. As we read the narratives about the Exodus in the Hebrew Bible, it becomes clear that the freeing of the Israelites from Egypt is not for themselves alone. Time and again God explains that this crucial event is meant to be seen and understood by the Egyptians as well, and indeed by all the other nations of the world. God is on the side of liberation, of movement and of change, not just for Israel, but for all God's creatures.

So our life is a kind of perpetual journey: from the known to the unknown, from the habits and conventions of today into the mystery and demands of tomorrow. And yet paradoxically wherever we go, whatever new situation we enter, we still remain ourselves, carrying with us all the habits and patterns, burdens and knowledge of our past. We are never free of our past, but, as the Exodus theme suggests, we can use our past in a constructive way. By studying it, re-enacting it, we come to recognize how far it still affects us and limits us. Rather than deny what we have been or have done in the past, we try to learn from these experiences. So by repeating the cycle of our festivals, by reflecting on our own past life as individuals and as a people, we can see how far we are still trapped in old patterns of behaviour, and how far we have actually moved on. So the cycle of the Jewish calendar is not simply an endlessly repeating circle but rather a kind of spiral, taking us round the same events again but from a new perspective, leading us further on our actual journey.

This idea of journeying back to ourselves so as to progress is reflected in many different sources. There is a chasidic story, common to many other cultures and traditions, that is recounted by Martin Buber. It concerns Rabbi Eizik, son of Rabbi Yekel of Cracow:

He was a very poor man, but nevertheless retained his faith in God. Once he dreamed that someone told him to look for a treasure in Prague, under the bridge which leads to the King's palace. The dream came to him three times, so he understood it as a message from God and set out for Prague. When he arrived he found that the bridge was guarded day and night so he did not dare to start digging. He went to the bridge every morning and kept walking around it until evening. Finally the guard who had noticed him asked in a kindly way whether he was looking for something or waiting for somebody. Rabbi Eizik told him of the dream, but the guard laughed: 'So you wore yourself out coming here for the sake of a dream! If I believed in dreams I'd have made my own journey. I once dreamed that I should go to Cracow and dig for treasure under the stove in the house of a Jew called Eizik, son of Yekel! I'd have had to try every house there since half the Jews are called Eizik and the other half Yekel!' Rabbi Eizik said goodbye to him, returned home, dug up the treasure from under the stove, and built the House of Prayer which is called 'Reb Eizik Reb Yekel's *Shul*'.

But dreams are not confined to the past or to the legends of the chasidim. A friend of mine, an Orthodox rabbi, told me about a couple of dreams he had had. In both of them he was an actor in a play. But though the play in the second dream was completely different, he began to realize that all the actors were the same as those in the first dream. When he thought about it he realized that the dream had come at a time when he was having difficulties with his congregation and contemplating moving on to somewhere else. He now realized that the dream was telling him that wherever he went he would encounter the same kinds of people and the same kinds of problems – so it was better to work them out where he was and not simply run away.

Both these dream stories suggest that here where we stand is where our treasure is to be found, the answer to the riddle of our own personal life and destiny. And yet, in order to find that treasure, we may have to go on a long journey.

They remind me of another variant on this theme of the journey that was told to me many years ago by a very special woman. She too spent her whole life on a religious quest, searching for intellectual and spiritual integrity and freedom. She died a few months ago and this is a kind of memorial to her. Her name was Gisela Hommel, and through her writings and radio broadcasts in Germany, she did much to explore contemporary religious issues. She raised her voice in protest at many trends in Christian theology in Germany which she found mistaken or destructive. She was a life-long student of Jewish teachings and fought for a better Christian understanding of Judaism. Gisela's father had been Jewish but had died just after the advent of the Nazis, so her family arranged for her to be brought up under a different name in another part of Germany. For many years she studied Judaism with Rabbi Yehudah Ashkenazi and was a regular participant, and occasional lecturer, at the annual Jewish–Christian Bible Week that is held each year at the Hedwig Dransfeld Haus in Bendorf near Koblenz. She talked from time to time about the possibility of formally converting to Judaism, but felt that she had a task to fulfil as a Christian in educating the church about Judaism from within.

Once she described herself as like a housewife who made the sandwiches and did all the preparations so that the family could go off on a trip somewhere. When the bus left she had to stay behind to do the clearing up and the housework. But one day, she said, she too would run after the bus and catch it! Gisela has now caught a different kind of bus, but she leaves behind, amongst all the housework, an important collection of writings and teachings that reflect her own special journey.

The journey from slavery to freedom is not easy. At the first sign of difficulties the children of Israel attacked Moses and told him to leave them alone. Slaves who live in fear of their lives, fear change even more. As Rabbi Nachman of Bratzlav put it, 'Whoever stops to ask about provisions for the journey, will never get out of Egypt.' So the story of the Exodus is not simply a comfortable legend to recount – it is a call to courage, imagination and will. It is a challenge to undertake a journey that may have great risks, but it will lead us back in some way to a better understanding of ourselves and the chance for yet another new beginning. Franz Kafka describes in his own unique way both the mystery and the exhilaration of this journey into the unknown:

I gave orders for my horse to be brought round from the stable. The servant did not understand me. I myself went to the stable, saddled my horse and mounted. In the distance I heard a bugle call, I asked him what this meant. He knew nothing and had heard nothing. At the gate he stopped me, asking: 'Where are you riding to, master?' 'I don't know,' I said, 'only away from here, away from here. Always away from here, only by doing so can I reach my destination.' 'And so you know your destination?' he asked. 'Yes,' I answered, 'didn't I say so? Away-From-Here, that is my destination.' 'You have no provisions with you,' he said. 'I need none,' I said, 'the journey is so long that I must die of hunger if I don't get anything on the way. No provisions can save me. For it is, fortunately, a truly immense journey.'[1]

[1] Franz Kafka, *Parables and Paradoxes*, Schocken Books, New York 1961, p. 189.

HARDENING PHARAOH'S HEART

(*Va'era* Exodus 6.2–9.35)

Towards the beginning of our *parashah* this *Shabbat* comes a sentence that continues to shock us, as indeed it must have shocked generations of readers of the Hebrew Bible. Moses and Aaron have attempted to persuade Pharaoh, the King of Egypt, to let the children of Israel leave the country. But their intervention has actually made matters worse for the Israelites. So they complain to Moses and Moses complains to God. When God responds it is to explain that there is more at stake in the present events than just the freeing of the children of Israel, and more even than finding them a homeland. God intends to multiply the signs and wonders that take place in Egypt so that the Egyptians too come to recognize the power of Israel's God. But to achieve this God will harden the heart of Pharaoh (Exodus 7.3) so that he does not listen to Moses, and that will provide the opportunity for God to unleash all the plagues.

God's actions seem to be very unfair on Pharaoh. If God is hardening Pharaoh's heart, how can he be blamed for refusing to listen to Moses' words or accept his warnings. And if the Egyptians are to suffer the plagues because of Pharaoh's stubbornness that becomes doubly unfair. Furthermore, what about Pharaoh's freedom of choice if God is simply manipulating him?

The rabbis struggled with this puzzle. In one view Pharaoh

himself had set certain things in motion through his actions. He was the one responsible for the death of many Israelites. He had been given a number of opportunities to repent through the warnings that came with the first plagues. But there came a time when punishment was inevitable and God caused it to happen by hardening Pharaoh's heart so that he was no longer willing to change.

On this reading we do have freedom of choice – but only to a certain extent. Once we take a particular course of action and various consequences are set in train, these generate their own dynamic. We too become caught up in a series of events that in turn force us to continue in the same direction. So we become even more stubborn and unyielding. That is why the Bible sometimes says that God hardened Pharaoh's heart and sometimes that Pharaoh hardened his own heart. He became caught up in his own pride and unable to escape the momentum of the events that he had generated.

Behind these events that are described in the Bible there was also a kind of psychological warfare going on between Pharaoh and Moses. Pharaoh's response to Moses' request to let the people go was to punish the Israelites. In that way he caused a split between Moses and the people he was trying to help. Moses became blamed for making things worse and that could have been the end of his attempts to mobilize the people. God had to reassure Moses that this too had been foreseen and was part of a divine plan. So the plagues were used to regain the initiative and, in fact, to play Pharaoh's game back against himself. As the plagues became increasingly more dangerous, first Pharaoh's advisers, then the people ceased to obey him and took their own measures to protect themselves and ensure their survival. In the end Pharaoh was totally isolated and completely out of touch with the needs and circumstances of his people. The struggle was not just with Pharaoh but with the structure of his society that gave such power into the hands of one man.

Even then, when the sensible thing would have been to let the Israelites go and get on with rebuilding his damaged kingdom, Pharaoh could not do so. And in chasing after the Israelites he led his army to its destruction in the mud and waters of the Sea of Reeds.

There is something very familiar about Pharaoh's attitude. We have seen it in the dictators and tyrants of every century, including our own. They share a certainty in their own right to rule and a willingness to sacrifice everyone and everything to maintain their power. This may even lead to destroying the very people they claim to love and serve. The political problem and the psychological truth of the Exodus story are disturbing warnings to each and every society.

The Israelites saw in the events the hand of God. We may be reluctant today to make such a direct assumption when it comes to the actions and final downfall of the dictators of our own time. Instead we are horrified to witness the endless suffering of the victims of tyranny, and the seeming hopelessness of attempts to remove those who abuse their power. The plagues are equivalent to the boycotts and sanctions we use to topple unpopular or dangerous regimes today. But it is usually the common people who suffer while a Pharaoh continues on his own way. Sometimes everything has to be destroyed before a Pharaoh can be persuaded or forced to give up power.

Whether we read this story in terms of God's intervention to harden Pharaoh's heart, or see it in psychological terms alone, the reality of such attitudes is all too familiar. We need constant vigilance to ensure that our systems of government do not allow power to be held and abused in such a way.

Rabbi Akiva addressed the question of our freedom of will by simply stating the paradox under which we live. He said: 'Everything is foreseen, but freedom of choice is given.' We are neither totally free in what we do nor totally bound. If we try to be honest with ourselves we can anticipate the consequence of much of what we do. It is then up to us to choose whether to harden our hearts or find another way to act. That is our extra-ordinary human gift and our daily challenge.

LAW AND LORE

(*Bo* Exodus 10.1–13.16)

This week's *parashah* contains a verse of extraordinary importance for Jewish tradition. It occurs at the beginning of chapter twelve of the Book of Exodus:

> The Eternal said to Moses and to Aaron in the land of Egypt: 'This month is for you the head of the months, it is the first for you of the months of the year.'

Though it does not seem to be particularly significant, it is quoted by the great mediaeval Bible commentator Rashi in his very first comment on the Book of Genesis. Rashi tells us that according to a certain Rabbi Isaac the Bible should not have started with Genesis at all! It should really have begun with Exodus 12 verse 1.

According to Rabbi Isaac the whole of the creation story, the tales of Abraham, Isaac and Jacob and Joseph could all have been left out of the Bible. Clearly he is trying to be provocative and immediately he brings his own explanation for why the Genesis stories are included. People sometimes accused Israel of taking the land of Canaan from its inhabitants. But, says Rabbi Isaac, the Genesis stories tell us that God created the whole world and so is entitled to decide who gets which part. As long as Israel behave in the right way, they are entitled to the land. But why did Rabbi Isaac think that the Bible should have started with Exodus 12?

The answer he gives is that this is the first commandment given by God to the entire Jewish people. Before they even reached Mt Sinai where they entered a covenant with God, they received and accepted this law about the Passover. For Rabbi Isaac the essential thing about Judaism is not the stories of the Patriarchs, however worthy they may be, but rather the giving of laws, *mitzvot*, to Israel. The centre of Judaism for him, is *Halachah*, Jewish law. Anything else in the Bible is largely irrelevant unless a reason can be found for it.

It may be that I am being unfair to Rabbi Isaac by suggesting that he was making *Halachah* into such an absolute thing. In fact his teaching may have been meant ironically, at the expense of those who considered only *Halachah* to be important.

After all, only a small part of the Hebrew Bible consists of law. The rest is made up of all sorts of materials – stories, history, prophetic sayings, poetry and prayers. The term that is used to describe all of these materials is *Aggadah*, which comes from a verb *l'haggid*, meaning 'to tell'. We are more familiar with it in the form *Haggadah*, the special book giving the order of service of the Passover evening home ceremony. *Aggadah* is used by the rabbis to describe 'lore', whatever is not legal material in their commentaries on the Bible.

If the rabbis weave a story around an unusual sentence, or try to read between the lines of a conversation, or try to explain why someone acted in a particular way, or point out some kind of moral, all of these and many more examples come under the heading of *Aggadah*. If the rabbis ask what happened to Abraham during the three days journey on his way to sacrifice Isaac and then fill in the details of his inner struggle – that is *Aggadah*. If the rabbis speculate on what life will be like after death, or when the Messiah will come – that is *Aggadah*. If they try to understand the suffering of the Jewish people and illustrate their ideas by telling a parable about a king who had a son and sent him away as a punishment,

then the king is God and the son is Israel – and that is also
Aggadah.

So *Halachah* and *Aggadah* are complementary to each other,
each providing something that the other lacks.

Time and again we find when we look into Judaism that it presents us with two opposing ways of seeing things or acting in the
world. All too often we fall into the trap of taking sides – if one
view is correct then the other must be wrong. But this 'either/or'
approach is destructive; Judaism teaches us to find the middle
way, to live within these contrasts and transform them.

Judaism is based on a covenant with God, and a covenant is a
legal contract which puts obligations on both partners. Israel's
task is to create a society based on justice and mutual respect and
that is the purpose of much of the legislation in the Hebrew
Bible. But though laws can do a lot to regulate society they only
touch on part of our life. Human relationships are built on a
complex mixture of feelings and emotions, duties and responsibilities, so Judaism has a structure based on law but what holds
it together is all the complex human emotions that we call love.
That is why the rabbis taught that God was also to be known
through two contrasting characteristics. The *middat ha-din*, the
quality of pure justice, balanced by the *middat ha-rachamim*, the
quality of love, mercy and compassion. Wherever you touch
Judaism these two forces are to be found. Whether we call them
Halachah and *Aggadah*, justice and mercy, or law and love,
Judaism speaks to the whole of our life.

SLAVE OR FREE

(*B'shallach* Exodus 13.17–17.16)

This week's *parashah* begins in a curious way. After the successful defeat of Pharaoh by the ten plagues, the children of Israel march triumphantly out of Egypt. One of the opening sentences seems to emphasize this – the children of Israel went up '*chamushim*' from the land of Egypt. What is the meaning of this Hebrew word *chamushim*? It seems to derive from the number *chamesh*, five, and it is generally assumed that they went out in some kind of military formation based on the number five. Hence some translations read that they went up 'armed' or 'equipped for battle'. But the previous sentence conveys a very different impression. It explains God's perspective on this exciting moment: 'God did not lead them through the land of the Philistines, which was the nearest route, for God thought that when the people saw the possibility of war they might change their minds and turn around and go back to Egypt!' (Exodus 13.17).

So we have here a kind of tragi-comic picture. The Israelites themselves go out brandishing weapons, suddenly feeling heroic because they have been given freedom. But God knows that beneath this bravado, they are still slaves at heart, their spirits broken by their past experience. At the first sign of trouble their courage might collapse. This had happened once before in Egypt. When Moses first asked Pharaoh to let the people go, he had not only refused but he had made conditions worse for the Israelites.

In this way he succeeded in driving a wedge between the people and Moses. At that time they had confronted Moses and said: 'You have made us stink in the sight of Pharaoh and you have put a sword in his hand to kill us!, you have given him a pretext to destroy us.' But Pharaoh was already killing their first-born sons, and hardly needed an excuse! For a slave any change is somehow threatening and dangerous.

There is an ironic little joke that exactly describes this kind of fearful mentality – it is literally a case of gallows humour (*Galgenhumor*). Two men are standing in front of a firing squad waiting for the command to shoot them. One of them turns to the other and says: 'Do you think I could ask for a cigarette?' The other replies: 'Shhh – don't make trouble!'

God sees through the apparent courage of the Israelites marching in formation out of Egypt and decides not to take a risk with their new-found confidence. In fact, as the story develops, we know that almost all of this generation that has come out from Egypt will not enter the promised land at all. Instead they will die in the wilderness during the forty years of wandering.

The great mediaeval Jewish commentator Abraham Ibn Ezra explained the reason why that generation could not enter the promised land. In their hearts they were still slaves and lacked the kind of courage needed to conquer the land. Instead the children of Israel had to wait till a new generation had been born in the desert as free people, able to face hardship and tackle difficult situations, before the next step could be taken.

Only Moses was truly free. He had been brought up in the court of Pharaoh so he had lived a life of independence and freedom. Moreover he had been groomed for leadership. Yet he could have simply stayed within his Egyptian palace and led the life of an Egyptian prince. What led him back to his people and a very special destiny?

An episode in his early life reveals something of his character and helps explain why he acted as he did. In the familiar story, when Moses grew up he

> went out to his brothers and saw their burdens and he saw an Egyptian man striking a Hebrew man, one of his brothers. (Exodus 2.11)

We tend to assume that when he went out to see 'his brothers', it is the Israelites that are meant. But again Abraham Ibn Ezra forces us to look more carefully at the passage and asks why the word 'brother' comes at the beginning and again at the end of the sentence. Moses has grown up as an Egyptian. His last contact with his Jewish origins ceased when he was weaned. At the burning bush he will not even know the name of his ancestral God! So when he goes out to see the burdens of his brothers, it is as an Egyptian prince that he goes out to see the burdens of his Egyptian people. For the Egyptians are indeed burdened with their huge building projects (Exodus 1.11). But at the moment when Moses witnesses the brutal striking of a slave, despite all the assumptions of his royal upbringing, he intervenes on behalf of the victim. At that point he identifies who is truly his 'brother', whoever is the victim of oppression. Moses becomes an Israelite only after he has discovered his compassion and sense of justice.

At the beginning of the *parashah*, Moses has succeeded in the first part of his task. The children of Israel are setting out on their way to freedom. But there is a major contrast between Moses and the Israelites at this moment. For Moses takes the time to collect the bones of Joseph and ensures that they are taken with the Israelites when they depart (Exodus 13.19). He was fulfilling the promise that Joseph had extracted from his brothers. That when Israel left Egypt they would take his bones with them for burial in the promised land (Genesis 50.25). Moses makes sure that this promise to Joseph is fulfilled. While the Israelites are acting as if they were warriors, Moses, the only real warrior among them, remembers their spiritual responsibilities.

Perhaps we see here a further sign of the slave mentality. Once freed, slaves can remain trapped in the violence that has been done to them. So they in turn may do violence to those in their power and not even recognize or acknowledge what they are doing. They may also come to believe that brandishing swords and making threatening gestures is the way to show their authority, that aggression and force can resolve conflicts. While the Israelites think of weapons, Moses thinks instead of Joseph. He was sold as a slave by his brothers but he had the inner strength to seek reconciliation with them. Joseph had been treated as a slave but never became a slave.

So, filled with these inner tensions, torn between slavery and freedom, at once outwardly triumphant, but fearful within, the children of Israel set out on their journey to the promised land.

WHY JETHRO?

(*Yitro* Exodus 18–20)

This week's *parashah* is named after Jethro, the father-in-law of Moses. He comes to meet Moses in the wilderness after the children of Israel have escaped from Egypt. The *parashah* is called by Jethro's name in Jewish tradition simply because his name appears in the opening sentence, and this is the usual way in which the *Torah* readings are referred to. Chapter 18 of Exodus begins:

> And Jethro the priest of Midian, the father-in-law of Moses heard all that God had done for Moses and for Israel His people, for the Eternal had brought Israel out from Egypt.

What was it that Jethro had heard that made him come to greet Moses? That is a question asked by Jewish tradition and we will come back to it later. But meanwhile something else is very puzzling about this *parashah* which covers three chapters of the Book of Exodus. Chapter 18 describes the meeting between Jethro and Moses, and then Jethro's suggestions for a restructuring of the organization of the camp. Too much of the burden of leadership rests on the shoulders of Moses and he needs to delegate authority to others. Jethro could be adopted as the 'patron saint' of management consultants!

All of this is very interesting, but it does not prepare us for what is to come next. Chapter 19 contains the awesome account of the revelation at Sinai and the agreement of the children of

Israel to enter into a covenant with God – the single most important event in Israelite history after the Exodus from Egypt itself. And if that is not enough, the following chapter, chapter 20, contains the text of the Ten Commandments, the crucial summary of the religious and social values of the Hebrew Bible, and indeed the Jewish, Christian and Muslim civilizations that are to arise from it. In dividing up the Bible into sections for reading in Synagogue, the rabbis could have started this particular *parashah* with chapter 19, the revelation at Sinai. So why did they choose to start with chapter 18 instead? The result is that these important events and texts are forever remembered by the name of Jethro, someone who was not an Israelite and who even belonged to a different religious tradition?

Before suggesting a possible reason, I would like to tell a personal story about Jethro. But for Jethro my parents might never have got married and I might never have been born! My father was born in Canada. As the child of immigrants from Russia, he had an Orthodox Jewish upbringing in a town called Glace Bay in Nova Scotia. While he knew a lot about Jewish customs and traditions, and felt very much at home in the Synagogue, he had not done much in the way of traditional Jewish studies, like so many of his generation who had to make their way in the new world. He became a doctor and came to England at the beginning of the Second World War where he met my mother and wanted to marry her. So he was introduced to her family and one *Shabbat* he went to synagogue with his future father-in-law. My father was introduced to the rabbi who said to him: 'I have heard a lot about you, Dr Magonet.' At which point my father suddenly remembered a phrase from Jewish tradition that he had heard in his childhood. It comes from our *parashah*. Not from the Bible itself, but from the commentary of Rashi, the great mediaeval commentator. Since our chapter begins: 'And Jethro heard', Rashi immediately asks: '*Mah shemua shama* – What was it he heard?' When the rabbi said to my father that he had heard all about him, without thinking, my father found himself quoting the words of Rashi, and he said: '*Mah shemua shama* – What was it he heard?' From that moment on everyone was convinced that my father was not only a doctor but also a great Jewish scholar! What a husband he would make! So if that moment helped my parents to get married, then I truly owe my existence to Jethro.

But let us return to the broader question of why the rabbis felt it necessary to link the name of Jethro to these important chapters about the revelation at Sinai and the Ten Commandments. One of the reasons may be precisely because Jethro is not an Israelite, but instead a representative of the outside world. When Jethro says that he has heard what God has achieved in bringing Israel out of Egypt, he represents the nations of the world and their reaction to this incredible event. On their behalf he acknowledges the liberating power of Israel's God. In the same chapter Jethro will even recite a blessing to mark the event:

> Blessed be the Eternal who rescued you from the hand of Egypt. (Exodus 18.10)

So Jethro becomes also the first to acknowledge in public the religious significance of the Exodus from Egypt and to sanctify it with a blessing.

The presence of Jethro at this crucial moment is a reminder that the Exodus from Egypt, the liberation from slavery, has universal significance. Moreover Jethro also acts as a bridge to the next event, the revelation at Sinai, that sets a seal upon the Exodus.

At Sinai Israel entered into a covenant with God. Central to the covenant are the rules and regulations that are meant to create a special kind of society, one built on justice, mutual respect and love amongst the people. The Exodus defines the universal nature of human rights, that no-one should be enslaved to someone else or to a system. It is the right to live in freedom. But the covenant at Mt Sinai demonstrates the limits set on our personal freedom. We exist in relationship with other people as part of a human community. So the covenant defines the universal nature of human duties and responsibilities. The presence of Jethro as an outsider who witnesses these events means they are not just for Israel alone. Israel is to be the instrument whereby these values, of freedom joined to social responsibility, are to be transmitted to all of the peoples of the world.

So once again we return to our opening question: What was it that Jethro heard that made him make the journey to visit Moses? On one level the answer is quite domestic, and related to my father's experience. After all Moses was Jethro's son-in-law, the father of Jethro's grandchildren. He had gone away on this dangerous mission and was now returning. Jethro needed to know what had happened to Moses and try to bring him back to look after his family. No wonder he was shocked that Moses spent the whole day seeing people and judging cases. Where was he to find time for his wife and children?! Jethro may have given advice like a good management consultant, but he was also acting out of the love and concern of a father-in-law.

But there was clearly a deeper level to his interest, as a religious man who shared many beliefs with Moses and with the Israelites emerging from their years of slavery. Jethro made his journey to witness this extraordinary phenomenon and experience at first hand the power of this God who had defeated the might of Egypt and its gods. Jethro too wanted to share in the journey of this people, even if only for a short while. So Jethro becomes also a reminder that the world is not just a hostile place. That the religious journey is not just a solitary one. And that the Exodus from Egypt, together with the covenant made at Sinai, freedom together with responsibility, are a challenge to all people at all times and in every place. *Mah shemua shama.* That is what Jethro heard.

CLOTHES MAKE THE MAN

(*Tetzaveh* Exodus 27.20–30.10)

Our *parashah* comes from the last part of the Book of Exodus and includes a description of the clothing to be worn by Aaron the high priest. It explains in extraordinary detail how each piece is to be made with precious materials and with the greatest of craftsmanship. It is clear that each garment has its own special significance and symbolic value: the breastpiece, ephod, robe, embroidered tunic, turban and girdle (Exodus 28.4). Together this clothing is to indicate the special task of Aaron, to sanctify and to honour him, to set him apart as a Priest of God.

The description reminds us that clothing has always been used as a way of indicating distinctiveness and difference. Our clothes mark out where we belong in a particular society, or indeed whether we belong to that society or not. We take this so much for granted that we sometimes forget that the basic purpose of clothing is not display but protection. But from the very beginning clothes have had the additional function of concealing or revealing parts of our body, of indicating where we stand in a particular hierarchy or simply of attracting attention to ourselves. Clothes provide a message to the rest of the world about who we are. So it is no surprise that themes associated with clothing occur throughout the Hebrew Bible.

They begin with the story of the Garden of Eden when Adam and Eve first discover their nakedness. The word *arumim*, naked, is used elsewhere in the Bible for people who are weak and defenceless – such as newborn children or captives being led away naked into exile in the land of their enemies. So when Adam and Eve discover that they are naked, their concern is not first of all their sexuality, as is so often assumed, but rather their awareness of their weakness and vulnerability. They have eaten of the tree of knowledge, but what have they learnt? How defenceless they are! In Eden they were like children under the protection of loving parents, who shielded them from all dangers and difficulties. They had no knowledge of the dangers that the world contained. Now that they are out in the world alone, they understand for the first time the price they must pay for their independence. So when God provides them with clothes it is a way of extending the divine protection to them. God is available if we wish to ask for help in this way.

But clothes mark also different stages in our life. In the story of Joseph clothes play an important role. We think at once of the 'coat of many colours' given him by his father, Jacob. The Hebrew term refers to a kind of cloak worn by royalty, so the cloak is a sign of the high esteem in which his father holds him. But this coat is stripped off by Joseph's brothers when he is cast into the pit. As a slave in Egypt Joseph serves Potiphar in a new garment – but Potiphar's wife strips this off him as well when she tries to seduce him. In prison Joseph has another garment, but this too will be replaced by royal clothing when he comes to serve Pharaoh. The acquiring and shedding of his clothes symbolize the different status he has in society each time and the ups and downs of his life.

Even more dramatic is the symbolic use of clothing in the tragic story of the conflict between the prophet Samuel, King Saul and David. When Samuel tells Saul that he will no longer be king, Saul tears Samuel's cloak and this symbolizes that the king-dom will be torn away from Saul. David will later cut off the edge of Saul's robe, which marks the beginning of Saul's defeat.

Jewish tradition is aware of the significance of clothing – the practical need for protection and the symbolic way in which clothing reveals things about us. We are instructed in the Ten Commandments to 'honour' our father and our mother, and the rabbis understood this to mean that we should make sure that they have adequate clothing, as well as providing them with food and shelter – the three basic essentials for life. They extended this idea even further and, based on the Adam and Eve story, they taught that we should also try to follow the example of God – just as God provided clothes for Adam and Eve, so should we try to provide clothing for the naked in our own society.

This year marks the fiftieth anniversary of the death of the great German Jewish Bible scholar, Benno Jacob. It is just over sixty years since his monumental commentary on the Book of Genesis was published in Germany. Tragically it was destroyed by the Nazis almost as soon as it appeared and only a few copies escaped. Because of this, his very detailed and important analysis of the text of Genesis did not become part of academic Bible study there. Benno Jacob writes about the significance of clothing, especially that of the priests, and how it marked them out for their higher calling to serve God. But he comments also on the clothing that God gave to Adam and Eve:

> The fact the the Lord Himself gave Adam and Eve garments and clothed them indicates that clothing is not just a social convention but an extension of the work of creation, a kind of second skin given to man, a nobler material encasement.

According to Benno Jacob, the clothing of Adam and Eve is like the clothing of Aaron – it symbolizes their rising to a higher state than that of animals, with a particular identity and an individual task. As Moses dresses Aaron for his vocation as high priest, so God dresses Adam and Eve for their vocation as human beings.

We are a long way away from the time when Israel had a Temple and a high priest. Clothing does not identify certain kinds of Jew as sacred – but it does still indicate different religious and social positions. Different chasidic groups have their own distinctive dress. The struggle by women to have a recognized place in Jewish worship is symbolized by whether or not they wear a *tallit*, a prayer shawl. The kind of *kippah*, skull cap, you wear on your head indicates something about where you stand in the Israeli religious scene (black satin for the ultra-orthodox, 'knitted' for 'modern orthodox' and infinite varieties between and beyond). There is also an old joke about the American Jewish scene – an Orthodox Jew always wears a *kippah*; a Reform Jew never wears one; and a Conservative Jew keeps one in his pocket!

The rabbis were very aware of the social implications of clothing and the status it can confer upon a person. The English proverb says: 'Clothes make the man', but the rabbis had their doubts about this. They said, 'When a rabbi comes to town he is judged by what he wears. But when he leaves the town, he is judged by who he is!'

LIVING WITHOUT A TEMPLE

(*Tetzaveh* Exodus 27.20–30.10; Ezekiel 43.10–27)

Today's *Haftarah* from Ezekiel chapter 43 is part of the prophet's vision of a new Temple in Jerusalem. In exile in Babylon, he remembers still Solomon's magnificent Temple that had been destroyed by the Babylonian conquerors. Now his vision shows him in the greatest detail just how it is to be rebuilt when the people return.

The Temple in Jerusalem is one of the most potent of the Biblical images. It represents the presence of God in the centre of Israelite society. The sacrifices that took place there every day gave expression to all aspects of Israel's worship.

The private individual who had sinned in some way and damaged his relationship with God could bring a sin-offering and find forgiveness. Those who had experienced some joyous event in their lives or had been rescued from danger, could bring a thanksgiving sacrifice and give public witness to God's actions in their life. The nation as a whole could mark the seasons of the year through the great Festival celebrations, praying for the success of the coming harvest and giving thanks to God at the end of the year. These great pilgrimages to Jerusalem also gave a sense of unity and purpose for the people as a whole.

But temples are never simply spiritual places alone. To create a sacred space within, they need to have vast, solid walls around them. It is as if they have to strike a balance between the spiritual and the material, and the material always threatens to overwhelm the prayers and offerings that take place within. The Temple in Jerusalem symbolized the power of God, but also the power of the King who was God's regent on earth. And where there is power there is potential conflict – between the King and the Priesthood, between church and state – and the Temple in Jerusalem was often the focus of such political struggles.

The Temple was also a storehouse – not only of spiritual values but also of the material wealth of the nation. In its treasuries were kept the booty won from war, alongside the gifts dedicated to God. And these treasures that belonged to God often had to be made available for very secular purposes in times of political or military emergency.

Temples are expensive places to maintain. They need to be kept clean and repaired. It cost vast sums to support the priests and levites with their families, those who slaughtered the animals or sang in the choir, who taught the people their tradition or policed the building and its sacred precincts.

Because the Temple was at the centre of the religious life of the nation, it became the focal point of major issues about the values and priorities of that society. Today we sometimes put religion into a special place in our lives, a higher more spiritual part. But Israel's God had entered into a contract with them to create a just society here on earth. For Israel, religion could never be divorced from the quest for justice and the struggle with the realities of power. Personal piety could never be separated from political action.

And where there is power and conflict, there may inevitably also be corruption. The sacrificial system could express the willingness of each individual Israelite to offer themselves and all they had to God. But that same system could be reduced to a mechanical way of covering up guilt or pretending to seek forgiveness from God without a real inner change. For some it could be just a kind of public display, as the rich vied with each other to show off their wealth and piety. Prophets like Isaiah and

Jeremiah attacked the entire Temple apparatus and administra-
tion for these faults. Isaiah condemned people who had made
their money by exploiting others then came piously to the temple to offer their sacrifices. Not only was such activity hypocriti-
cal, it brought the whole relationship with God into disrepute.
Jeremiah saw a people blind to the injustices in their society who
believed that the Temple would save them from all harm. He
mocked their magical faith in 'The Temple of the Lord, The
Temple of the Lord, The Temple of the Lord' (Jeremiah 7.4).

Solomon's Temple was destroyed. It was rebuilt by those who
returned from exile and magnificently extended by King Herod,
only to be destroyed by the Romans. It had been central to
Israel's religious life for over a thousand years, so how did
Judaism survive without it?

Today's reading from the Book of Ezekiel reflects this problem. For those of his generation who were in exile in Babylon,
their hope of returning to their land was linked to the Temple.
How could they come so close again to God without the Temple
as the centre of their spiritual lives? Ezekiel's detailed vision of
how the temple would be rebuilt must have given them hope of
restoration

But Ezekiel also gathered around him the leaders of the exiled
community. It may be that in those circles there developed the
activities that would eventually replace the functions of the
temple and transform their religious life.

Somewhere in exile they began reciting prayers to coincide
with the times of the daily sacrifices, and this became the new
way of communicating with God. Within those prayers were
allusions to the temple ritual so that some sort of continuity was
maintained. Study of the *Torah*, the laws of the covenant and all
the related traditions, became a new way of seeking the will of
God in their lives. From these early beginnings emerged a new
kind of spiritual leader, the rabbis, and the system of a priestly
hierarchy was replaced by the democracy of learning. Even the

symbolic furniture of the temple, God's house, took on a new meaning in the exiled community. The family home became the *mikdash me'at*, the 'little sanctuary'. The altar became transformed into the family table; the father officiating at the domestic rituals replaced the priest.

When the second Temple was built by the returning exiles it contained a room for prayer and places for study. When Herod's Temple was destroyed by the Romans, its replacement, the Synagogue, was already in existence.

There is a great message of hope in Ezekiel's vision. It is possible to lose all the old religious landmarks so that it seems as if there is only a memory or vision of them left to hold on to. But the human spirit is greater than that, and within the destruction itself it is possible to find the seeds of renewal. But what is needed is a willingness to confront the mistakes of the past honestly, and seek in the most direct and open way, the new word of God for a new time.

Ezekiel is told that he may only describe his vision of the new Temple if the people are ashamed of their past faults. Temples to God can all too easily lose their religious integrity. The material can overwhelm the spiritual; faith in God can be reduced to magical thinking; and power and authority can slip into exploitation and corruption. No religious system is guaranteed. So we never lose the task of examining the holy temples of our lives and continually seeking within them the presence of God.

MOSES THE FUNDRAISER

(*P'kudei* Exodus 28.21–31)

When people turn to religion today, it is often because they are looking for something different in their life. They may have found that the materialism that surrounds them is empty of values or that success, as the world seems to see it, is not really enough. So they turn to religion for comfort or even an escape from their daily concerns. While some religious traditions may seek to lead us away from the practicalities of life, Judaism tends to do the opposite. It is very committed to this life and its realities – but it tries to discover the religious point and value in everyday activities. A good example comes at the beginning of this week's *parashah, P'kudei* (Exodus 38.21–31) which deals with some very businesslike matters.

Many of the previous chapters in Exodus have been taken up with a detailed account of the building of the tabernacle in the wilderness. Now that the work is completed, Moses has one more task to perform, just like any other person in charge of a major public works project. He has to prepare a balance sheet, draw up an income and expenditure account of the entire operation, and conduct a financial audit. The responsibility for organizing this is given to Ithamar, the son of Aaron the priest.

The Bible is quite precise about the money involved. The currency used in Bible times consisted of small pieces of gold or silver that were valued by their weight – the basic unit was the *shekel,* and three thousand *shekels* made a '*kikar*' or 'talent'. So people would carry around with them a silver or gold ornament, or small bars or pellets of the metal, and weigh them out when they made a transaction. A lot of such transactions are recorded in the Bible, such as when Abraham buys a grave in which to bury his wife Sarah, or David buys a site for the Temple. Since this kind of currency depended on the accurate measurement of weight, some kind of standard measure had to be used for comparison. This was kept in the sanctuary and later the temple. It was called the *shekel ha-kodesh*, the sanctuary *shekel*, and our text points out that all the weights of gold and silver that are recorded here were measured against that guaranteed standard.

When Ithamar presented the audited accounts for public scrutiny, he was able to report the following:

> All the gold that was used for the work of building the sanctuary … came to 29 talents and 730 *shekels*, checked against the sanctuary *shekel*. The silver donated by those of the community who were recorded (in the census) came to 100 talents and 1,775 *shekels*, checked against the sanctuary weight; that is a half-*shekel* per person for each one who was entered in the records from the age of twenty years up, 603,550 men. (Exodus 38.24–26)

That was the income side of the balance sheet. Part of it, the silver, was obtained by direct taxation, the half *shekel* that each adult male had to give when presenting himself for the census. But the other part, the gold, and the bronze, came from voluntary donations. Whenever someone made a sacrifice, a contribution went to the building work as well.

Ithamar now presents the expenditure side of the account – and this too comes with great detail:

> The 100 talents of silver were used for casting the sockets of the sanctuary and the sockets for the curtain, 100 sockets cost 100 talents, one talent per socket. With the remaining 1,775

shekels he made hooks for the posts, a silver overlay for their tops and silver bands around them.

Such statistics may not seem very interesting or of great religious significance. But anyone who has taken responsibility for fundraising for a synagogue building or other charitable project might well recognize some familiar challenges here. How much money can you get from the congregation by direct levy? How much do you hope to raise by donations from rich members, and how much from smaller gifts from other members? If my own experience of fundraising for good causes is anything to go by, there are some unexpected questions we may have to ask. Did Moses have to put on fundraising dinners in the desert? Did he have to invent special honours for people to encourage them to give more money, or publish their names on a list of 'major donors'? We have to remember that only a few chapters earlier, the Israelites were volunteering to give their golden earrings to help build the golden calf. To make a second appeal for money after such a short time is never easy!

Our passage leaves out a lot of things that we would be interested in knowing today. Did Ithamar draw up the budget for this major building project? Did the fundraisers reach their target? Did the builders, as so often happens, go over-budget and have to economize on parts of the building? Was there a group of people who complained that a sanctuary was the last thing they needed in the wilderness and that the money raised would be better spent on weapons to defend themselves, or on better food for the journey, or an education programme for their children? If these are not the usual questions one asks about a biblical passage, they are nevertheless important, because they help bring the reality of the issues to life.

Certainly the rabbis looked very carefully at what was going on. They saw a major problem with the fact that God put Moses in sole charge of the project. They were very concerned about the accountability of public officials. They taught that at least three people had to be in charge of public funds, so as to lessen the chances of mistakes or fraud. That was the reason, they explained, why Moses immediately appointed Ithamar to be in charge of the finances – that way Moses could share the responsibility but also make it clear to the people that everything was in order.

Financial accountability and honesty is a major concern in rabbinic thought. At the centre of the Book of Leviticus is the chapter that begins: 'You shall be holy because I the Eternal your God am holy' (Leviticus 19.2). Just before the end of the chapter come the laws about weights and measures. The word *tzedek*, which means 'righteousness', appears here in its basic sense of something that is 'just', 'consistent and reliable'. Its fourfold repetition comes like a hammer blow emphasizing its tremendous significance:

> You shall do no wrong in measurements of length, or weight or quantity, *moznei tzedek avnei tzedek eifat tzedek v'hin tzedek.* You shall have just balances, just weights, a just dry measure and a just liquid measure. (Leviticus 19.35–36)

The whole of human civilization depends on the integrity and reliability of weights and measures. If these cannot be trusted then all possibilities of commerce and fair dealing disappear. The rabbis taught that someone who uses false weights and measures is the worst of sinners and in great trouble with God because he or she cannot do *teshuvah*, repentance. In order to repent you have first of all to make amends to people for the wrong you have done them – but someone with unreliable weights can never find out who he has wronged and to what extent!

I began by suggesting that sometimes we come to religion to get away from these daily considerations of business. But Judaism forces us to look for the religious truth in such seemingly mundane things as keeping a proper record of money transactions and being honest in our business dealings. Moses and Ithamar showed that those in public office have an even greater responsibility and their record has to be open to public scrutiny.

But if some Jews come to synagogue to escape from worldly concerns, it seems that others do the opposite. A rabbi once complained to his congregation: 'People spend so much time in synagogue talking with each other about their business in the market place – if only they would devote as much time during their business hours in the market place talking about God!'

SPRING

TWO KINDS OF SLAVERY

(Shabbat Chol Ha-Mo'ed Pesach)

At *Pesach*, Passover, we celebrate our liberation from the slavery of Egypt. The symbols of the *Seder*, the home ritual on the first two evenings of the festival, illustrate this transition from slavery to freedom. They are summarized in the *Mah Nishtanah*, the passage read out by the youngest child at the *Seder*, who asks, 'Why is this night different from all other nights?' The child offers four things that are different and therefore puzzling.

'On all other nights we eat either leavened or unleavened bread, but on this night only *matzah*, unleavened bread?' The slave has no choice but must accept whatever food is available. But the unleavened bread is to remind us of the haste with which we were forced to leave Egypt. It is the food of the refugee, the last thing that is grabbed as you rush out the door, on the way into exile and an unknown future. As the *Pesach Haggadah* describes it: *ha lachma anya*, 'this is the bread of poverty.'

The second question also emphasizes the experience of slavery. 'On all other nights we eat any kind of vegetables, but on this night only *maror*, bitter vegetables?' The bitterness of slavery is recalled, of lives wasted and empty of meaning; the bitterness of powerlessness in the face of brutality and slow death.

But the other two questions present the contrast. 'On all other nights we do not dip even once, but on this night we dip twice?' The reference is to dipping a vegetable into salt water before eating it and later on dipping the bitter herbs into the sweet *charoset*, a paste made of apple, wine and cinnamon which symbolizes the mortar used in building the Egyptian cities. But dipping food into different spices or condiments also points to the luxury of a meal eaten at leisure, when an *hors-d'oeuvres* before the main course is served. Freedom is here measured by the quantity and quality of the food available to us and the amount of time we have available to linger over it and savour it.

The same image of a luxurious feast is echoed in the last of the four questions: 'On all other nights we eat sitting or leaning, but on this night we all lean?' This fourth example was a late addition to the set of questions after the Temple was destroyed. It replaced an earlier text about eating the special lamb that was sacrificed for the Passover meal. Without the Temple this practice had to be discontinued, so the question about leaning was introduced. It was borrowed from the practice of the Romans who used to lie down on couches as they ate their meals. It was the Romans who had destroyed the Temple. Now their victims borrowed this symbol of freedom and power to demonstrate their true freedom under God.

So the four special activities of this Festival meal reflect two radically different situations: the unleavened bread and bitter vegetables symbolize slavery; the luxurious food and relaxed eating speak of freedom.

We are called upon to remember the experience of slavery, to taste it in our mouths. For only if we know slavery can we appreciate and understand the value of freedom. We need to use our imagination on this night. As the *Haggadah* tells us. In every generation everyone is obliged to regard themselves as if they had personally come out from Egypt. We become truly Israel by experiencing the fate of Israel at the time when it became a nation.

As on so many other occasions in our Jewish tradition, we are asked to remember our past. But to remember it in a creative way, make it actual, present, part of our lives today. In fact the

Hebrew word *zachor*, to remember, contains that idea. In some of its grammatical forms it means to speak, to proclaim, to make an event or an idea or an experience become real, actual or present in the world. Remembering the Sabbath day means more than just a casual memory that there is such a thing as the *Shabbat*, it is to keep the *Shabbat* at the forefront of our consciousness throughout the week. Remembering means for Judaism that we are always living in a present moment that is informed by the past. The past is alive within us. We are the people that remember.

So what exactly is it that we are to remember on the Passover evening? Firstly, the experience of slaves. Indeed the Hebrew Bible reminds us time and time again that we should remember that experience in Egypt so that we do not inflict upon others the suffering we experienced ourselves. We who have known the soul of a slave must never impose that bitter suffering upon another.

But the *Pesach Haggadah* tries to define the idea of slavery a bit more precisely. And indeed there was an early rabbinic debate about what slavery means which is preserved in the pages of the *Haggadah* itself. The rabbis had an ancient tradition that in telling the story of the Exodus on the *Seder* night we should begin the telling of our experience with something shameful but end with something praiseworthy. The thing that was shameful was our experience of slavery, the praiseworthy thing was that God brought us out to freedom.

But why is slavery described as shameful or disgraceful? Clearly it was a bitter experience, but to be the victims of oppression is not something to be ashamed about – if anyone should be ashamed it should be the Egyptians for reducing a people to slavery. So two rabbis came up with different solutions about what constituted our disgrace. One felt that it was indeed the experience of physical slavery and the low level to which we were reduced. But another one wanted to go further back into our history and recall that Abraham was once an idol-worshipper, so that our origins were pagan. This slavery to false gods was for him the really shameful part of our past.

As is so often the case, the tradition came to a compromise position and preserved both views. That is why the *Haggadah* refers to both events and we have the passage beginning: 'We were slaves to Pharaoh in Egypt …', but also the passage: 'At first our ancestors were idol-worshippers …'.

So when we celebrate the Passover we are challenged to examine slavery on two levels – the physical and the spiritual. At times when we have been physically enslaved as a people, we have always been able to discover within ourselves a spiritual freedom that helped us not only survive, but also remain true to our inner Jewish experience and values. In one of the concentration camps the question was asked whether it was right to recite the morning blessing in which we thank God for not making us a slave, *shelo asani aved*. How could that prayer be said in all honesty when the inmates of the camp were clearly slaves. But the answer was given that it was more important than ever to recite such a blessing – because it asserted that whatever the physical slavery to which they were subjected, they were still spiritually free.

But in a time when we are not physically enslaved, the question of our spiritual freedom must also be examined. What are the values or ideas that enslave us today as Jews? Sometimes we are actually trapped by precisely that thing which we consider one of our greatest virtues – our ability to remember. Sometimes our memories of our tragic past, especially the destruction of this century, actually paralyse us when we have to act in the present. We remember our Egyptian slavery so well that we do not always see the freedom and responsibilities that we carry today.

So perhaps the tradition was very wise when it insisted that these questions of the *Seder* night are to be asked by the youngest child. It is the duty of the parents to give answers, to instruct, but unless the child asks questions nothing can happen, the festival service cannot even begin. At the very moment when we are asked to remember, to bring the memory of the past into the present, we are warned that the past can also be a trap. We can also be enslaved by memory unless we are able to listen to the urgent questions of a new generation. They look with puzzlement and scepticism on the rituals, traditions and values that they see around them. They ask their hard questions because they have to be convinced of the worth of what we hand on. So a place must be made for them to ask, and the way we listen and answer will determine whether the tradition survives into the next generation. When we cease to listen to the questions of our children, then our past can become an idol and we can become its worshippers. When we cease to question ourselves about how we use our memories of what has happened to us, then our past can become a prison, and we truly become its slaves.

LOVE SONGS TO GOD

(*Chol Ha-Mo'ed Pesach* – Song of Songs)

This *Shabbat* falls in the middle of *Pesach*, the Passover, between the first day which celebrates the departure from Egypt and the seventh day which commemorates the crossing of the Sea of Reeds. It is an extraordinary moment. Behind us is the great event of liberation from slavery but before us the barrier of the sea which blocks our way. And somewhere in the distance we can hear the rumbling sound of Pharaoh's chariots in pursuit. It is a time to move on as fast as we can to escape the danger that threatens to overtake and destroy us. And yet Jewish tradition has chosen this moment to pause and read from one of the most controversial books of the Hebrew Bible, the Song of Songs of Solomon.

Each of the three Pilgrim Festivals is associated with a special book but the links are not always clear. Certainly the Song of Songs refers to the springtime so it fits this season well – just as the Book of Ruth, read at *Shavuot*, Pentecost, speaks of the barley harvest. But why pause at this moment to read the words of a love song, one that was almost excluded from the Bible altogether?

The Bible itself offers a few clues. When the prophets criticized the Israel of their times, they looked back to the period of the Exodus and the wandering in the desert as a golden age. They saw it as a time of courtship and love between God and Israel. Like a bride following her husband into a new life, so Israel was willing to trust God and journey into the unknown desert. The prophet Jeremiah expresses it in a phrase that he may have repeated whenever he spoke in public:

I remember the faithfulness of your youth,
the love of our bridal days,
when you went after me into the wilderness,
into a land unsown. (Jeremiah 2.2)

So if that moment was an expression of love, what is more appropriate to celebrate it than a love song? But what kind of love song?

The Song of Songs is problematic for many religious people precisely because it is so sexually arousing. It is sensuous and erotic. It is explicit in its description of the bodies of the two lovers and the physical desire they have for each other. And the Song weaves feelings and emotions together with imagery so powerful that you can smell the perfumes that surround the lovers, taste the sweetness of their kisses and feel the urgency and the heat of their bodies as they embrace.

What is particularly strange about its inclusion in the Bible is that it seems to contradict the sexual modesty and conventional morality of other passages. Some scholars suggest that the Song looks back to the kind of ideal love that existed in the Garden of Eden before Adam and Eve were expelled. It was a time when the first man and woman were truly equal, exactly complementing each other, and when physical and spiritual love were intimately bound together. After the expulsion from Eden these aspects split apart and sexuality became distorted by a new relationship between women and men based on dependency and power. So the Song celebrates all aspects of the experience of sexual love, the meeting of senses and imagination, of emotions and physicality, of spirit and body, and it looks forward to the restoration of this wholeness.

This sensitivity and complexity would also explain how the

Song came to be understood in purely spiritual terms as celebrating the love between God and Israel. For human beings are
made in the image of God and the descriptions in the Song
became transparent in the imagination of mystics seeking union
with the divine.

But the explicitness of its sexual content also led the Song into
less obviously spiritual places. It became popular in the taverns
in the times of the rabbis and according to Jewish tradition it had
to be rescued from them by the great Rabbi Akiva. He alone saw
its spiritual importance despite the crude way in which it was
understood and treated. So intensely did Akiva feel its power that
he made the famous claim that though the rest of the books of
the Bible were 'holy', the Song was the 'holy of holies', the most
sacred expression of religious faith and love.

So the Song remains full of massive contradictions, accurately
reflecting our own uncertain attitudes to human sexuality, an
area of fear and disgust for some, of physical pleasure and joy
for many and a source of creative and spiritual inspiration for
others.

Reading the Song of Songs at *Pesach* is appropriate in many
ways. At this festival that celebrates liberation and freedom it is
important to consider the way people enslave and abuse each
other, and how so much of our human interaction is distorted by
the power games we play. The Song of Songs reminds us that
God would have us meet as equals in the most public and most
intimate parts of our lives. And the spiritual dimension of the
Song, the love and loyalty that transcend our physical existence
and even the finality of death, gives us a glimpse of how we can
grasp in our own lives the passionate love of God.

> For love is strong as death
> jealousy is cruel as the grave
> its flashes are flashes of fire
> a flame of God. (Song of Songs 8.6)

YOU ARE WHAT YOU EAT

(*Shemini* Leviticus 11.45–47)

If you ask people what they know about Judaism, one of the things they are sure to tell you is that Jews don't eat pork. Though this is just one small part of the complex dietary laws of Judaism it has impressed itself on the popular mind.

Why is this so? It may be because of the obvious social difficulties it raises. Breaking bread together is the most basic and natural part of human community. Any dietary system that interferes with that is a challenge to human solidarity – and it is inevitably a source of misunderstanding and resentment. So it is important to try to understand the reasons behind the dietary laws – if we can discover what they are.

The verses we read today from the third book of Moses (Leviticus 11.46–47) come at the end of a chapter that lists a variety of forbidden animals. They sum up the chapter: 'This is the law concerning the beasts, birds and all living creatures that move through the waters and every creature that swarms upon the earth, to make a distinction between the unclean and the clean and between the living creature that may be eaten and the living creature that may not be eaten.'

The reason why the Israelites may not eat these particular animals is not given. Some rabbis even taught that these are laws given by God whose reasons we are not to know. They are to be obeyed because God gave them and that is the beginning and end of the matter – needless to say, this has never stopped other rabbis speculating about the reasons for them.

One explanation may indeed have something to do with social mixing. The animals the Israelites were forbidden to eat might have been sacred to other nations or used for some idolatrous religious practices. These laws were given to prevent the Israelites being influenced by these practices and the people who performed them. For example, in the Book of Genesis, the Egyptians would not let Joseph eat with them because he ate foods they considered sacred and forbidden. But it is not clear why the Israelites could accept some aspects of the culture around them but not others. So the separation factor can only be a part of the story.

In the nineteenth century, when the pioneers of scientific medicine began to understand more about the transmission of disease, it was realized that pig meat, unless very carefully cooked, could be the source of disease. So there arose a theory that the dietary laws were really about hygiene. Certainly the biblical priests were also doctors and must have had a lot of practical knowledge about illness. But, once again, this hygiene theory does not explain all the animals that are forbidden.

We can look at the problem from an entirely different point of view. When God chooses the sons of the patriarchs, He rejects the hunters and chooses instead those who are shepherds. Both Ishmael and Esau are hunters and are put aside in favour of Isaac and Jacob who keep flocks and herds and work the land. If we now look at some of the animals that are permitted and forbidden, it is clear that the *Torah* encourages the Israelites to eat animals that feed on grass and which are raised and kept by human beings. Excluded are animals that hunt others or that scavenge. There was an American saying some years ago that was popular among hippies: 'You are what you eat.' The Israelite is to be chosen for domestic values, for farming, for building societies – not for hunting and killing. So even the food we eat should reinforce this idea.

There is yet another recent explanation that comes from anthropology. If you look at the laws in this chapter, they give certain principles to help you recognize which animals you may eat. For example, fishes must have fins and scales; animals must have a split hoof and must chew the cud. But then Leviticus lists a number of animals that are specifically forbidden. These include those that have some of the permitted characteristics but not all of them – so they are halfway in and halfway out. This leads to a theory that the Israelites, or at least their priests, saw that God had created a universe that was very carefully separated into different parts. For example, there were three domains in the world: the sky, the earth and the sea. Israelites were allowed to eat fish, but not shellfish that lived partly in the sea and partly on land – they crossed a boundary between two domains. In the same way, some animals like cows and sheep had the right physical characteristics. But although pigs had split hooves, they did not chew the cud, and so they had to be excluded. They crossed two domains. This suggests that there are ideal divisions in the natural universe, deliberately created by God. The Israelites had to show their own wholeness by acknowledging and aligning themselves with the separate categories God had made. The act of eating, that was so essential for life, should be dedicated to fulfilling God's wish for these correct distinctions.

That would also explain why our text here talks about 'clean' and 'unclean' animals. These words are a poor translation of the Hebrew terms *tamei* and *tahor*. They do not mean physically clean in the hygienic sense. They really describe states of existence that make it appropriate to be in the presence of God. If they conform to the ideal pattern of the universe, they are 'clean'. But if they do not conform they are 'unclean', that is to say, 'inappropriate'. In the same way human beings could become unfit at certain times in their lives because of bodily discharges, or because of contact with a dead person. In such circumstances they would have to stay outside the camp for a certain period and then return after a ritual cleansing.

This same way of classifying things leads to distinctions within time as well – so that there are six days for working and a seventh day for rest. It is a way of organizing and controlling human existence, perhaps to find some sort of security in a chaotic universe.

Which of these explanations for the Jewish dietary laws is right? Perhaps all of them contain part of the truth, but the rabbis were probably right in thinking that we will never know for sure.

Let us ask instead, what are the lessons we can learn from them? In the Jewish Grace that we recite after the meal, there are four separate blessings through which we thank God for the food we eat. But each of those blessings can also teach us about an important responsibility that we bear.

The first one ends: 'Blessed are You, our living God, who gives food to all.' It is a reminder that God provides ample food for everyone in the world – but that we are God's agents to make sure that everyone receives the food due to them. We are obligated to produce a society and a world in which no-one should starve.

The second blessing ends: 'Blessed are You, our living God, for the land and for the food.' This is an early warning that we must care for the earth itself which gives us so much but which is so easily abused and destroyed.

The third blessing concludes: 'Blessed are You, our living God, who builds Jerusalem.' Many Jewish prayers focus at some point on Jerusalem. It is a symbol of our task to help build God's kingdom here on earth. The rabbis taught us to be aware that enormous numbers of people had to collaborate with each other just to bring food to our tables. We should never take this for granted. We are all part of a chain of mutual human responsibility. Even in our choice of food we are making judgments about who we buy from, what sort of societies we wish to support and the welfare of those who provide so much for us.

The final blessing describes God as one who does good to all. It reminds us that for us to eat, other living creatures must die. For that privilege that is given us, we are responsible for seeing they do not suffer either in their lives or in their way of dying.

We have moved a long way from the biblical verses with which we began – but not really so far. We too must be concerned with what is clean and unclean, *tamei* and *tahor* – not in terms of dirt or hygiene, but in terms of our behaviour: what is right and appropriate for us to do if we accept that what we eat is a gift of God and that we eat it in the presence of God.

ONE HUMANITY

(*Kedoshim, Haftarah* Amos 9.7–15)

The *Haftarah*, the prophetic reading for this *Shabbat*, is taken from the book of Amos, chapter 9, the closing verses of his book. They speak words of consolation to the people after all the warnings that the prophet has given of destruction that will come to his society if it does not change its values. But the beginning of our section (verse 7) is one of the classical prophetic challenges to biblical Israel.

> Are you not like the Cushites to me, O children of Israel, says the Eternal. Indeed I brought Israel out from the land of Egypt, but I also brought the Philistines out from Caphtor and the Arameans from Kir.

In this assertion that God intervenes in the history of all peoples, we seem to have the second part of a conversation between the prophet and his contemporary Israelites. Someone must have said, 'God loves us more than all the nations of the earth. Look at our marvellous tradition, how God set us free from slavery in Egypt and even now cares for us with a special love.' Of these religious half-truths Amos is highly critical.

What makes you think you are so special? God has intervened in the history of all the nations around you as well. That alone is no reason to think of yourselves as better than others. It is the way you behave that will determine whether God treats you in a special way. And if your society is corrupt, God will surely destroy it, whatever the special relationship you think you have.

Amos seems to be pointing to the gap that so often exists between what we know in our minds as civilized, cultured people and what we actually experience at the level of our intuition and emotions. In Amos' time, even a schoolchild would have known that Israel's God was the creator of the whole universe. Such a child would have been able to tell the stories of Adam and Eve, of the great flood and how Noah saved the world by building his ark. And how his three sons went out and repopulated the entire world again. So all human beings come from the same one man, Adam, and all are equally God's children, each special to God in their own way.

But knowing that as a religious teaching and truth, or even as a scientific reality, is not enough. It is quite another matter to accept it at a deeper emotional level, in the face of the differences between peoples and nations and races and religions. Because over and above all our nice theologies and rational explanations are some very basic, unrefined feelings about who 'we' are and who 'they' are; about what belongs to 'us' and what belongs to 'them'; about whom we love because they are like us, and whom we fear and mistrust and even hate because they are different. We are somehow capable of having a magnificent, universalistic view of the One God, creator of heaven and earth, the all-merciful protector of every human being, and yet at the same time still have the most crude, tribalistic sense of God as somehow belonging exclusively to us. And all too often it is our emotional feelings of our differences that overwhelm our reasoned awareness of all that we have in common. Our God fights on our side alone, in a world exclusively ours.

A part of me would like to stand up like some ancient prophet and say how awful this is, and demand that we live up to the high universalistic ideals of our faiths. But I think we need today a little less preaching and rhetoric about such things and a greater commitment to understanding what goes wrong in human society. We know so much about the psychology of prejudice and stereotyping and scapegoating – it is time we did the work on ourselves in changing our behaviour towards those we consider as different. That is perhaps the greatest religious challenge we face today, and certainly the one on which our religions will be judged in the future.

Jewish teaching, in direct continuity with the thought of Amos, is particularly explicit about the unity of all human beings. In the Mishnah, one of the earliest collections of rabbinic writings, we find the following teachings:

> Only one man, Adam, was created in the world to teach that if anyone causes a single soul to perish, Scripture considers him as having caused a whole world to perish. And if anyone saves alive a single soul, Scripture considers him as though he had saved a whole world.
>
> Only one man, Adam, was created for the sake of peace among human beings so that no-one should say to his fellow: 'My father was greater than your father' ...
>
> Only one man, Adam, was created to proclaim the greatness of God. For when a human being makes coins in one mould they are all alike; but God has formed everyone in the same mould yet none of them are alike. Because of this everyone should say: 'For my sake the world was created.' (Mishnah Sanhedrin)

But sometimes we can only learn the truth of the unity behind the seeming diversity of human beings through our own personal experience of suffering. Someone who came to such an understanding was Professor Eugene Heimler, whom I was privileged to know as a teacher and a friend. He died in 1980 and I am pleased to have this opportunity to evoke his memory

and teaching. He was born in Hungary, was a Jewish victim of
the *Shoah*, and survived a number of concentration camps
including Auschwitz. After the war he wrote about his experiences in the camps and about his long and painful journey
back to normal life. As a psychiatric social worker, he pioneered
new methods for helping people understand their lives and their
own particular, unique journey. He made a point of visiting
Germany after the war and teaching there, despite all that he had
suffered, perhaps because of what he had learnt through his
experience during the war. He wrote the following piece which
can be read as one of the most profound comments on the words
of Amos and the Jewish teaching about the essential unity of
humanity:

> It was in Buchenwald that I learnt from Jews, Christians,
> Moslems and pagans, from Englishmen, Serbs, Rumanians,
> Albanians, Poles and Italians, that I was only one more
> suffering insignificant man; that the tongue my mother taught
> me, and my Hungarian memories and the traditions of my
> nation, were nothing but artificial barriers between myself
> and others. For essentially, as Mankind, we are one. A slap in
> the face hurts an Englishman as much as it does a German, a
> Hungarian or a Negro. The pain is the same; only our attitude
> to the pain differs according to the cultural pattern of the
> country and the individual. Our dreams, each dreamt in a
> different language, spell out the same dream in the language of
> Mankind: all of us want peace, security, a life free from fear.
> And each in his own way, irrespective of differences of nation-
> ality or race, we seek for the meaning – or meaninglessness –
> of life and death, believe in God or deny him, cry for a woman
> on whose bosom we may rest our tormented head ...
>
> I learnt that within me, as in others, the murderer and the
> humanitarian exist side by side; the weak child with the vora-
> cious male. That I am not in any way superior, that I am not
> different from others, that I am but a link in the great chain,

was among the greatest discoveries of my life. From then on
I resolved to support those who fell, even as I had been
supported. When someone was despicable, greedy and selfish,
I remembered all the occasions when I, too, had been despic-
able, greedy and selfish. Buchenwald taught me to be tolerant
of myself, and by that means tolerant of others. It may be that
I would have learnt this without the lesson of Buchenwald.
But I would have learnt it much later – perhaps too late.

Between the words of the prophet Amos and those of Eugene
Heimler are two and a half thousand years of human experience
of the unity of humanity but also of the persistence of national,
religious and racial conflict. Though we know better, we nevertheless tolerate this human aberration in an extraordinary way.
Every religious tradition can express similar sentiments about
human unity – and the secular religions of our time, like human-
ism and socialism, can also match these ideas word for word.
That is the comedy and tragedy of our human aspirations and
hopes – our glorious vision and our shameful reality. So we will
continue to need the prophetic voices of Amos reminding us that
we are all of us special in the eyes of God and all of us equal. And
above all we will need the courageous witness of men like Eugene
Heimler who can draw out of their personal suffering a generous
and loving teaching open to us all.

CRITICIZING OURSELVES

(*Achavei Mot, Haftarah* Ezekiel 22.1–19)

The Hebrew Bible contains some of the most self-critical litera-
ture of the ancient world. Within it are preserved the most
scathing attacks on the behaviour and values of Israelite society.
In particular the prophets acted as the watchdogs and guardians
of public morality. Each in his own way drew attention to the
failures of the people to live up to their mutual responsibility to
one another under their covenant with God. Amos stood in the
market place and saw how the buying up of the land by the
wealthy brought poverty and misery to others. Isaiah, living in
the upper circles of the society, with access to the royal court and
to the Temple, saw the drunkenness of priests and prophets, the
arrogance of the generals, the dishonesty of the political leaders
and the bribery that affected the judges. But some of the
harshest and most uncompromising criticisms come in chapter
22 of the prophet Ezekiel, the *Haftarah* that we read today in
synagogue.

The prophet lists the sins of the leaders of Jerusalem, a city
which he says is full of blood because of them. The range of their
crimes is wide. They include sexual crimes – adultery and incest
– and this accusation is the link with Leviticus chapter 18 which
is part of the *Torah* reading for this *Shabbat*. But he also condemns their mistreatment of the poor, the widow and orphan,
their taking of bribes, the corruption of the law courts, their
breaking of the Sabbath and abuse of the sacrificial system.

To these he adds their lack of respect for their parents so that we are reminded almost word for word of the laws of Holiness that are found in Leviticus chapter 19. So on one level, Ezekiel is attacking real crimes and sins that he saw in his society. But at the same time he is building his criticism on the laws, and even the exact language, that belong to his tradition, the covenant between God and Israel.

This makes it difficult to know whether we are to understand his criticisms in a literal way. Did the people really commit these acts that he condemns? Or is he using the traditional language symbolically, as a way of drawing people's attention to the wrongs in their society and the way in which their behaviour is offensive to God?

If it is difficult to be certain about what was really happening so long ago, how are we to understand this powerful attack when we read such passages today?

One approach is to look at them in their context. To see in this description of a corrupt society the real situation of Jerusalem in the years before the Babylonian conquest when the city was captured and the people taken away. Jerusalem, by that reading, deserved to fall because of the evil that was within it. Perhaps the words of the prophet were preserved for us precisely because his warnings of punishment to come were shown to be correct.

Another approach is to take very seriously the idea that we have to learn from this past human failure. We can respond to the anger and despair of the prophet and look at what is happening in our own society. The exploitation of the poor, especially those who are foreigners, the abuse of public power, the shedding of innocent blood in the streets – all these are crimes that are still with us, in every large city in the Western world. Ezekiel reminds us that we shall be called to account for the crimes that we ignore, those that happen on our own doorstep.

But we cannot read about Jerusalem without thinking of the political scene in the Middle East and the problems that surround Jerusalem today. Jews, Christians and Muslims alike have great hopes and expectations of that city. The emotions that are invested in it are exhilarating, but they also demand a terrible price. In any other place we can accept the usual human passions, greeds, stupidities and failures. They are part of the normal fabric of everyday life. But they somehow become magnified out of all proportion when they happen in the 'holy city' of Jerusalem. So much so that the 'holiness' of Jerusalem is often its greatest curse. We invest it with impossible dreams and fantasies that can never be realised. Then out of our disappointment and frustration come bitterness, anger and violence. We get caught up in destructive emotions that are just as great as the hopes we once had. And out of our anger we act. Holy places encourage very unholy deeds.

Because Ezekiel's criticisms were recorded in the Bible, they also take on that extra religious dimension. They sound so absolute, so condemnatory, that they make it seem that God can only ever be angry with human beings. They also seem to offer no hope, only an inevitable punishment and destruction. And in a perverse way, that can be very appealing. Instead of offering our anger to God as a sacrifice and renouncing violence, all too often we use religion as a way of justifying and acting out our private hurt and anger on a vast public scale.

When we look around the world it seems as if religion is actually one of the worst sources of violence. Whatever its claims to bring God's love or justice into the world, just as often it brings hatred and injustice. Our own private anger can get hijacked by mass experience and be turned into a holy crusade. And soon the worst kind of human atrocities become committed and justified in the name of God.

So how can we read these words of Ezekiel in a way that does not feed on that inner violence within us? How can we understand and transform the anger of the prophet?

Firstly the prophet was not standing outside his society, as if he himself bore no responsibility for what was going on, as if his own holiness protected him. He shared the guilt, but was willing to play his part in changing the future. And this engagement, social, religious and political, gives real authority to his words.

Moreover, by expressing himself in the language of the covenant with God, Ezekiel was also reminding his people of their own values and all the hopes and promises that belonged to their religious tradition. Like all prophetic calls, the threat was always conditional. Destruction was not inevitable. There was always a chance to change, and transform their situation. If they would only change their behaviour, the way back to God was always open.

Violence and destructiveness are the other face of holiness and faith. And religion can serve either side. It can be harnessed for good or evil. That is why we need the words of the prophets. They challenge us to self-examination and self-criticism. They call us to measure what we do against the best values of our tradition. But they also demand that we look with clarity and honesty at what we are doing in our society at this very moment. For every city can be Ezekiel's Jerusalem, with blood flowing in the streets. And every city can be Ezekiel's Jerusalem, where all meet with God, the holiest place on earth.

FROM EGYPT TO SINAI

(*B'chukotai* Leviticus 26.3–27.34)

At the time when this talk will be broadcast [1995] I will be celebrating a very special event, the publication in Britain of a new
Jewish prayer book. The appearance of a new prayer book is
always significant, but this one has particular importance for me.
It marks the completion of a project of prayer book revision and
editing that has taken twenty-five years.

I was still only a student rabbi when I was invited to work with
my colleague Rabbi Lionel Blue in producing a preliminary set of
translations for a new edition of the Sabbath and Daily prayer
book for the Reform Synagogues of Great Britain. I had worked
with Lionel for some years in our youth movement trying to find
young people from different parts of Europe who were willing to
enter Leo Baeck College to study to become rabbis. We were concerned with the rebuilding of the European Jewish community
after the war and it seemed to us that the quality of the future
religious leadership was an essential issue. Lionel soon found out
that I liked to write poetry and songs, so when he was asked to
make the first translations for the prayer book he turned to me.
'You write songs,' he said, 'you can translate the hymns and
poems of the prayer book!'

That casual invitation began a collaboration that has lasted
till today, during which time we have produced a Sabbath and
Daily Prayerbook, one for the High Holydays and now the third
volume for the Pilgrim Festivals, *Pesach*, *Shavuot* and *Sukkot* –
Passover, Pentecost and Tabernacles.

Those of you who are only used to the Orthodox Jewish community may be surprised at the religious diversity and pluralism that exists within Judaism. In America there are major Jewish religious movements: Reform, Conservative and Reconstructionist. Britain has Reform and Liberal synagogues, and, of course, pre-war Germany was the home of the first Reform and Liberal Jewish movements. It is part of the tragedy of the destruction caused by the Nazi period that this rich diversity of Jewish religious expression, which offered a wide variety of possibilities for Jews to identify with their religion, has been severely limited in Continental Europe. It is only now, fifty years after the war, that new stirrings in this direction are beginning in some countries.

The new prayer book would be recognizable to Orthodox Jews because the major sections of the traditional services are preserved. What are new are the readings, meditations and songs that are introduced to help clarify the special ideas and values of each of the three Pilgrim Festivals. *Pesach* has a particular emphasis on liberation from slavery and the special responsibilities of freedom; *Shavuot* is a festival that celebrates the covenant with God and the revelation of God's word to the world at Mt Sinai; *Sukkot* reminds us of the wanderings in the wilderness and is therefore a metaphor for the precarious nature of life. It is also a very universal festival, so it speaks also of our responsibility to so many people who are refugees in today's world.

These ideas and lessons are present in the traditional service but they are not always very obvious to Jews who do not have a strong knowledge of their tradition. So it is our hope that the new prayer book will bring these understandings and values into the lives of our communities in Britain.

This *Shabbat* occurs towards the end of a special period of time, the seven weeks between *Pesach* and *Shavuot*, days known as the period of the counting of the *Omer*. In biblical Israel on the second day of *Pesach* they would bring an *omer*, a sheaf of the first fruits, to the Temple and then count the forty-nine days till *Shavuot*. But these weeks also coincided with the period between leaving Egyptian slavery at *Pesach* and standing before God at Mt Sinai on *Shavuot*. For the study anthology in our prayer book we decided to do something special with this period of time. We created a series of readings and meditations for each day of these seven weeks, so that we can follow this spiritual journey in our own lives as well.

In the first week, as we leave slavery behind, we can meditate on what it means to be a slave, and how the essence of freedom is that we can make choices in our lives. This is a great gift but also sometimes a difficult and a painful challenge. All too often we prefer to remain slaves in some way than grasp the freedom that is offered to us.

In the second week, out in the wilderness, we might experience the first doubts about what we have done. The security of slavery is now left behind and there are no guarantees about whether we will overcome the challenges before us. We have to face the way ahead of us and take responsibility for what we do.

In the third week we might lose our way. There are no sign posts in the wilderness, just the pillar of cloud and the pillar of fire that lead us on. These might be our dreams or visions, our hopes or our convictions, or our simple faith and trust in God. But at least we do have something to guide us however difficult the journey may be.

In the fourth week we have become used to the hardships of our journey. In fact our passage through the wilderness might have become quite mechanical. It is the journey alone that sustains us and the knowledge that we simply have to keep going if we are to reach our destination and not die in the wilderness itself. This can be a time of weariness and there are many temptations to give up.

But in the fifth week we catch our 'second wind'. We have

passed the point of no return and a new sense of energy sustains us because our destination is now that much closer.

The sixth week offers us a new kind of contemplation of the wilderness in which we find ourselves. Because the very emptiness of the desert allows us to paint upon it our own visions and ideas. The space around us becomes filled with our own imagination. In its silence and stillness we begin to hear that voice that is calling us to a special encounter.

As the seventh week arrives we begin to prepare ourselves for the meeting with God at Sinai. The strains of the journey are put aside and a sense of waiting and expectation comes over us. For the purpose of the journey will now become clear and we will learn the direction it is to take in the future. We are to become confirmed in our identity and our destiny.

So this *Omer* period can be a chance for renewal of our vision of our lives – a reassessment of the journey we have taken till now and the purpose that lies behind our individual existence. We too leave the slavery of our conventional lives and look again towards our future.

It is my hope that this new prayer book will help make these festival services come alive for my own community and for others who make use of it.

The theme of slavery and freedom that is so central to the Pilgrim Festivals has an echo in the Torah reading for this *Shabbat* and it is a fitting expression of hope for the future. In the opening section from Leviticus 26, God speaks to the children of Israel.

> I will walk in your midst, and I will be your God and you will be My people. I am the Eternal your God who brought you out of the land of Egypt, from being their slaves. I broke the bars of your yoke and I made you walk upright. (Leviticus 26.12–13)

THE SMALL PRINT IN THE
CONTRACT

(*B'chukotai* Leviticus 26.3–27.34)

With this week's *parashah* we come to the end of the Book of Leviticus. It is an exploration of the theme of holiness and contains one of the central commands and values of the Hebrew Bible and of Judaism: 'You shall love your neighbour as yourself.' Holiness is about the relationship that exists between people and the care with which they maintain that relationship.

But chapter 26 which we read this week, comes as something of a shock. There seems to be very little about holiness here, instead it is made up of a series of blessings and curses: blessings that will come to Israel if they obey God; but curses if they do not.

Behind this language is actually a legal document. These 'blessings and curses' correspond to the 'small print' that you can find at the bottom of any business contract. Both parties agree to work together, and then set out in the contract the conditions of their partnership. But suppose one or other of the partners fails to live up to the terms of the contract – then the contract contains a list of sanctions and penalties that come into force.

The curses in Leviticus are just such a section in the contract, the covenant, between Israel and God. And they are very disturbing to read. If Israel disobeys the laws of God then diseases will flourish in the land and enemies will invade and rule them.

If they still refuse to obey God then in successive stages more and more misfortunes will befall them. Under siege in their cities they will starve to death. Their çities and altars will be destroyed. Worse yet they will be taken into captivity in exile, where they will live a life of constant fear and anxiety.

It is a chilling warning of a situation of insecurity and terror. It is a situation that has been experienced all too often by Jewish communities in exile.

This detailed spelling out of punishment seems to reinforce the image of the God of the Hebrew Bible as a vengeful, angry God, always ready to punish the Israelites.

But on the other hand, a contract is a contract. Much of our life is about negotiations, compromises and agreements we make with others. The moment there are two people in the world, they have to examine their relationship with each other: how to share resources; how to respect each other's needs, property and personal space; how to define their mutual responsibilities to each other.

We build our relationships on the basis of trust and much of the time we hardly even think about this. But when things go wrong, when a crisis occurs, then we realize how fragile many relationships actually are, and how many unspoken problems exist between us. Groups of people who have coexisted for long periods can suddenly find themselves in violent disagreement with each other, and then discover that there is no proper framework for resolving their difficulties. Then emotions take over, demands are made for loyalty to one's own group and confrontation and conflict with the 'other' becomes almost inevitable. That is why it is so important that at the time when people do make an agreement with each other, when there is good will on both sides, that provisions for the future be made.

This applies not only to business agreements. Whenever there is a deep emotional commitment as well, such as when two people marry each other, then the terms and conditions need to be spelled out even more carefully. But a couple deeply in love may well resent this. They may not be able to imagine, or want to imagine, that they might one day change their minds and wish to separate. To talk about the practicalities of settling some possible future disagreement seems to undermine the very basis of their new relationship. Yet traditional wisdom has always led societies to make such provisions, especially where something so central to the community as marriage is concerned.

If all this seems to be a very negative way of looking at relationships between people, there is also a positive side, especially when it involves two people in love. Precisely because we know that there is a contract, and that contracts contain the possibility of being dissolved, both partners can recognize and accept the freedom that they have within the contract. In theory, at least, there should be no dependency or manipulation here when both are free to walk away. Their individuality and sense of responsibility are recognized and validated. They can build something together, but know that it will only work if they actually choose to stay together. It is not external pressures, even religious pressures, that hold them together in the end, but such mutual respect and loyalty as they can create between themselves. The contract also means that there is a structure and framework to use for dealing with problems that arise and one which can be turned to in times of tension or difficulty.

The sanctions in the contract, sanctions that they have both understood and accepted, are a kind of warning. But they are also a reminder of the value of what they have built together, the care with which they created their partnership and what they risk losing by dissolving the relationship.

Something of these ideas exists in our *parashah* as well. These 'blessings and curses' are expressions of love and of anger, so they remind us of the deep emotional bonds between God and Israel and the paradox of the God of the universe entering into a covenant with a human society. If God's love was given full reign it would be all-devouring; if God's anger was set free, it would be utterly destructive. Instead these emotions are contained within a ritualised language of warnings and graded sanctions. They are shocking threats because they are so graphic and real; but they establish boundaries and limits, and contain the promise of reconciliation and restoration.

In the end we also know that God cannot be contained within the pages of a contract. Israel, too, in all its diversity and complexity, can no longer be defined by the language and metaphors of Leviticus. But the emotional ties remain, the love and the anger. In Jewish history, pain and suffering, the lure of idols and the challenge of new loves have time and again threatened to pull Israel and God apart. But in bad times and in good ones the formal ties and sanctions and promises of the covenant have helped us freely and consciously to choose to remain bound to one another.

SUMMER

CRISIS IN LEADERSHIP

(*Shelach l'cha* Numbers 13.1–15.41)

This week's Torah reading describes one of a series of major crises that faced Moses in the wilderness. After the euphoria of the first stages of their journey to freedom, the Children of Israel had begun to understand the reality of their situation, its dangers and hardships. Questions of food and water for such a vast number of people became important. Also the sheer size of the encampment made it difficult to regulate, and Moses had to delegate some of his power and responsibility to others.

Now the people are about to enter the promised land but decide to send in spies ahead of them to check out what they will have to confront. From the point of view of the Bible, this is already a problem. Surely they should have trusted God who had led them so well so far – saving them from Egypt, even destroying the Egyptian army in the Sea of Reeds. What could they possibly have to fear with God on their side?

Well, like most reasonable people, they wanted to have some idea about what they were going to face. Much as they trusted in Moses and much as they believed in God, it is not wise to commit yourself to such a dangerous step without at least checking out the reality and the risks.

So the spies, representing each of the twelve tribes, entered the land and explored it. They came back and gave their preliminary report to Moses, before coming before the entire assembly of the people. The biblical text at this point is not altogether clear – and indeed many modern scholars find here evidence of two different versions of what happened, as well as some contradictions about which parts of the land they actually explored. Nevertheless it is possible to see here a continuous sequence.

First came the technical report to Moses and the army. Here a major division appeared between the spies. They all agreed that the land they were about to enter was fruitful and 'flowing with milk and honey' as Moses had promised. But, according to the military assessment, the inhabitants were strong, the cities were well fortified and there were even giants among the population. Against this military assessment, only Caleb ben Yefuneh, the representative of the powerful tribe of Judah, gave a dissenting opinion. He sided with Moses and affirmed that despite these problems, they could achieve a military success. Since the rest of the spies could not accept Caleb's view, no policy decision could be made at this level.

As so often happens in such political struggles, someone leaked a highly negative version of the report to the people. The word spread that the land was of poor quality, a place that eats up its inhabitants! And the military fears of the spies were also passed on – 'the inhabitants we saw were so powerful that we felt like grasshoppers in comparison with them!'

Once these rumours got round the camp total chaos broke out. The text of Numbers chapter 14 describes it very well. The leaders of the *edah*, the governing body of the people, started shouting at each other; all through the camp people were weeping and wailing. Everyone blamed Moses and Aaron and the leaders of the *edah* accused them of misleading the people and bringing them to their deaths in the desert. Some people even started talking about setting up replacements for Moses and Aaron to lead them back to Egypt.

In these circumstances some kind of impeachment proceedings were started against Moses and Aaron who had to defend themselves before a public meeting of representatives of the entire community, the highest popular assembly of their society. Moses and Aaron fell on their faces before them – that is to say, they submitted themselves to the judgment of the court. At this point the Bible records the speech in their defence by Caleb and Joshua bin Nun, another of the spies and someone who will one day succeed Moses as leader of the people. Instead of talking about the problem in purely military terms, they put the whole thing into its wider religious context. First they set the record straight about the marvellous quality of the land – don't believe the rumours that the spies have been circulating, it really is a land flowing with milk and honey. Then they tried to reassure the people about the threat posed by the inhabitants. Instead of speaking as military men, as Caleb had done before, it is Joshua who pointed out that as long as God was on their side they were bound to win. They should never be afraid.

But when it came to the vote, the people were not prepared to be swayed by these arguments. Moses and Aaron were convicted of misleading the people and sentenced to death by stoning. At this moment, when all seemed lost, God intervened, warning Moses that the people had rebelled too many times! Now God was intending to wipe out the people entirely and start again using Moses as the founding father. Only Moses' intervention prevented this taking place. Instead God responded to the very fears the people had expressed: they thought that their children would die here in the wilderness – well that would not be the case! It was the older generation who had not trusted God who were the ones who would die out during the next forty years of wandering in the wilderness. Only the next generation, the children born in freedom in the desert, would enter the land.

Unfortunately not all the people were convinced by this divine intervention. Some of them now tried to go up and conquer the land by themselves, without God's approval. And they were defeated by the local inhabitants.

This is a disturbing story for many reasons. As we read it, it is so presented that we are led to sympathize with Moses and Aaron against the people. After all, we, the readers, know that God and Moses have to be right. God has rescued the Israelites from Egypt and saved them from Pharaoh, why can they not be more trusting. Surely they should have faith!

But the philosopher and theologian, Emil Fackenheim, has pointed out that the fears of the people are actually very serious and legitimate, and have to be heard. When they talk about their worries about what will happen to their children, how they might die in this wilderness, we cannot just ignore their words. Perhaps in the past we could have simply accepted the story from Moses' point of view. But, argues Fackenheim, after the *Shoah*, when a million Jewish children died, we cannot read this passage in the same way any more. We cannot be silent when the lives of children are threatened. We must protest and we must act on behalf of any children, anywhere. When we read this story today, we can no longer simply accept the point of view of Moses or of God, we must argue against them and take the side of the people, even against God. We must stand in solidarity with the Israelites and their children. We know too much about the death of innocent children to read these texts in the same way as before.

Fackenheim would have us turn the story inside out. To read against the obvious meaning that is being offered to us, because our perception of events has changed.

In a way the whole episode of the spies is a reflection of the changed way in which we read our religious life. If we have some kind of religious faith today it is tempered with a certain amount of scepticism. We are too conscious of the reality of the world and its complexity to have any kind of simple faith about the future. And yet if all we had was scepticism, we would have died in the wilderness and nothing of Jewish tradition might have developed.

THE SPIES REVISITED

(*Shelach l'cha* Numbers 13.1–15.41)

This week we read in Synagogue about one of the most dramatic episodes in the history of the children of Israel. They have escaped from Egypt and met with God at Mt Sinai. They have journeyed to the brink of the promised land and, apparently, at God's command, they send in spies to determine what it is like and what obstacles stand in the way of acquiring it. So our *parashah* is named after the opening phrase *shelach l'cha anashim*, 'send out special men to spy out the land'.

However, of the twelve spies, ten of them bring back a negative report. Yes, they say, the land is very fruitful, but the cities are fortified, there are giants living there and it will be impossible for us to conquer it! Only two of the spies, Joshua and Caleb, are optimistic about the possibilities. When the people debate the matter in their national assembly the view of the majority of the spies is accepted. They will not be able to enter the land. Some people even suggest they should turn round and go back to Egypt. It looks as if the entire enterprise is about to fall apart. As a result that generation is condemned to wander for forty years in the wilderness till a new generation, born in freedom, has the courage to undertake the task.

Part of the problem may have been a general dissatisfaction with the leadership of Moses. Indeed, a few chapters later in the Book of Numbers there will be a rebellion against him. Moses did indeed order the spies to check out the military situation, but it is clear that that was not his main interest. Instead he seems to be totally intoxicated with the idea of this marvellous land itself, whatever the obstacles that may stand in the way. Every other sentence of his instructions to the spies begins with the phrase *mah ha'aretz*, 'and what of the land itself'.

> And you shall see the land, what it is like and the people who live upon it whether they are strong or weak, few or many. And what of the land itself on which they live, is it good or bad, and what of the cities in which they live, are they just encampments or fortified? And what of the land itself, is it fertile or infertile, are there trees there or not? Be strong and bring some of the fruit of the land. (Numbers 13.18–20)

When the spies return to report to Moses and the leadership of the people, they do indeed show something of the fruit of the land, and admit that it is a land flowing with milk and honey. But they do not share Moses' vision and instead give a long catalogue of the fortified cities and the power of the people who live there. It soon turns into a debate purely about the military possibilities. Caleb argues that they can conquer it, the others say they cannot, and the discussion reaches a kind of political stalemate.

Then someone leaks the negative report of the spies to the general population and things go from bad to worse. At the public meeting convened to discuss the issue Joshua now takes the lead and argues from a completely different perspective. Instead of speaking in purely military or political terms he calls upon the people to trust in God:

> If God delights in us. He will bring us into this land and will give it to us, a land which flows with milk and honey. Just do not rebel against God and do not fear the people of the land. (Numbers 14.8–9)

In the end Joshua will prove to be right. And indeed it will be under his leadership, after the death of Moses, that the people will successfully enter the land. So for the Bible it becomes a matter of trusting in God, and certainly not one of assessing military matters alone. Religion wins out over politics.

When Moses talks about this episode in his final testament, in the Book of Deuteronomy, he tells the story rather differently. According to him it was not God's idea to send out spies. God only agreed to something the people had proposed because they wanted reassurance. As Moses explains:

> You came to me, all of you, and said: Let's send men before us and search out for us the land and bring back word to us about the road we should take into it and the cities we shall come across. (Deuteronomy 1.22)

Their request is perfectly reasonable. No military operation can be undertaken without proper knowledge of the terrain and the opposition. So the reconnaissance of the spies was essential. But if the people had really had faith in God, especially after all the victories they had seen in Egypt and at the crossing of the Sea of Reeds, surely they should have just trusted that God would help them this time as well and tried to enter the land.

Life is rarely that simple. The proverb says: 'The Lord helps those who help themselves!', which means that we have to do our part and not simply leave things to God. Another saying is rather more cynical, but seems to fit the situation even better: 'Put your faith in God, but keep your powder dry!'

This passage from the Bible took on an added dimension today in the year when Jews everywhere are celebrating the fiftieth anniversary of the founding of the State of Israel. Here too the military and political and the religious issues are deeply intertwined. Jewish claims to a religious or historical right to the land are today examined in the light of ethical questions about how the State of Israel came into existence and at what cost to the local population. Today's Calebs and Joshuas still argue about whether the security of the State depends on military power

alone or whether there are new religious issues that have to be
addressed, particularly those values that call for dialogue and
compromise in the quest for a lasting peace. Paradoxically today,
it is sometimes the generals, like the late Yitzhak Rabin, who ask
the deeper religious questions in the quest for peace, while some
of the official religious leaders are uncompromising and seem to
expect military power and control to solve their problems.

It is no easier today to discern the will of God in such a situation than it was in the time of Moses. Nor do we have a Moses
today to tell us with absolute certainty what is the will of God
in this situation. We are left to take complete responsibility for
our actions, balancing the political against the religious, self-
preservation and security against a quest for justice and peace.

Today, we are the ones who are within the land, not outside it.
We are the ones perceived to be giants, living in our fortified
cities. But for this generation as well the call comes from God:
shelah l'cha anashim, 'send out special men to spy out the land'.
But this time the land they have to discover is the land of diplo-
macy, of reconciliation and of peace.

THE CHOOSING PEOPLE

(*Shelach l'cha* or *Korach* Numbers 13/16)

There are many tensions in Jewish life. One of the oldest and the one that has again become central is that between homeland and diaspora, between living in the land of Israel and living amongst the nations of the world. The Bible knows two diaspora situations – the slavery in Egypt and the Babylonian exile following the destruction of Jerusalem and the Temple. Both are understandably portrayed as negative experiences.

The Bible never makes clear why the children of Israel had to endure slavery in Egypt. However the biblical authors time and again insist that the Babylonian exile was a punishment for the sins of the people. To live in the land of Israel is a God-given privilege but one that carries with it great responsibilities. For the last two thousand years the Jewish people living in exile throughout the world drew comfort from the idea that however hard the experience of exile might be it was nevertheless something ordained by God, and, as the Bible promised, could be reversed at any time. Today, with the re-establishment of the State of Israel, homeland and diaspora coexist as two alternatives for Jewish life, each with its opportunities and challenges.

The tension between these two destinations for Jewish life is shown in this week's *Torah* portion, or rather in the question as to which passage we should be reading here in our diaspora communities. A few weeks ago we celebrated the festival of *Shavuot*, Pentecost. In Israel the festival is celebrated for one day only, but in the diaspora communities, following an ancient tradition, it is celebrated for two days.

The reason goes back to a period before we used calendars, and the times of festivals were determined by witnesses observing the appearance of the new moon. While the information could be available almost immediately throughout the land of Israel, it would take time before it could be relayed to countries in the diaspora. The tradition arose in diaspora communities of keeping a second day for these festivals, so as to make sure one had observed the festival at the right time. As a result there are sometimes minor differences in the calendar between Israel and the countries of the diaspora.

This matter is further complicated today because while Orthodox congregations in the diaspora retain the tradition of keeping a second day, many of the modern Jewish religious movements, Liberal, Reform and Conservative, have abolished this second day as an anachronism in the modern world where we know precisely the date of the festival. Moreover some feel it is particularly appropriate to keep only one day so as to identify with the way the festival is celebrated in the land of Israel. In this way homeland and diaspora are bound together.

All of which leads to the following problem for this *Shabbat*. In 1999, for example, the festival of *Shavuot* fell on a Friday. If you keep two days for the festival in the diaspora then, although the next day is *Shabbat*, the festival readings replace the normal *Shabbat* ones. So the cycle of *Shabbat* readings is delayed by a week in the following period. As a result, this week's reading will be '*Shelach l'cha*', the story in the Book of Numbers about the sending of spies to explore the promised land. But if you follow the Israel calendar, *Shavuot* only lasted one day, the *Shabbat* reading on the following day was not affected and so this *Shabbat* we would be one week ahead and read the portion *Korach* about the rebellion in the wilderness against the leadership of Moses.

This difference between the two readings is not a major problem. Later in the year we will double up some of the readings so that Israel and the diaspora are again synchronized. Nevertheless there is a curious irony about the clash of readings for this week since the two possible passages also reflect concerns about the relationship between homeland and diaspora.

If we read the passage from *shelach l'cha* from Numbers 13 we meet the well-known story of the spies. Moses sent twelve leaders of the tribes to explore the promised land. They brought back an enthusiastic report about the quality of the land and its fruitfulness. But they then added the warning that the inhabitants lived in fortified cities and seemed to them to be giants. There was no way they could possibly conquer it. Even though two of the spies, Joshua and Caleb, insisted that if God so wished they could succeed, the majority were against and some even suggested that the children of Israel should turn round and go back to Egypt. As a result they had to remain in the wilderness for forty years till that whole generation died out, which was another kind of diaspora experience.

But if we read the other passage from Numbers 16 we learn that after this and other crises, all the different groups that had some kind of resentment against Moses came together under the leadership of a man called Korach. Though each group had different motives one in particular offered a political challenge. Moses had promised to take them to a land flowing with milk and honey, they argued. Instead they had just left a land flowing with milk and honey, Egypt, and were now going to die in this wilderness. They threw in Moses' face his political manifesto.

The spies from their perspective were right. The land of Israel is a place that has to be won through enormous struggle. It is not easy to work the land itself and life there is dominated by political struggles, within the society itself and with neighbouring lands. But Korach's followers were wrong about life in the Egyptian diaspora. For the Israelites it was no land flowing with milk and honey, but a bitter place of slavery.

Today, as never before, the choice is open to every Jewish person. Where do we live out our personal destiny, in the homeland or in the diaspora? For most of us no external pressures force us to make our decision. It is entirely up to us.

That freedom of choice is not the case for so many other peoples today. Every week more and more are added to the millions of refugees created by the upheavals, tragedies and violent actions of the twentieth century. Each individual and family experience in their own way the pain of the loss of homeland and the fear and confusion of beginning anew in exile. For most of them the possibility of return is at best a distant hope. Shattered homes and scattered families and friends are the reality. Anger and hate at those who caused this horror may burn in their hearts for generations to come. Not for them an ancient biblical promise to return, or an understanding of the will of a passionate and jealous God to sustain them. As we read this week's portion, whichever one we choose, we are called to do whatever we can to alleviate this suffering.

So it is right that the particular tension between homeland and diaspora be reflected in our choice of *Torah* readings. Our religious traditions do not conceal or remove such tensions, but rather demonstrate and clarify them so that they impact on our daily life.

If we do not understand these tensions that pull us in different ways we feel ourselves to be tossed about and bewildered, even torn apart, by this strange Jewish identity that we bear. But if we can acknowledge their reality and understand the different forces acting upon us, then at least we are empowered to cope with them. That is the gift of freedom we obtained when we left the slave camps of Egypt. If this sense we are not the 'chosen' people, but truly the 'choosing' people. And we, the world and God, have to live with the extraordinary challenge that lies in that fact.

POLITICAL LEADERS ON
TRIAL

(*Korach* Numbers 16–18)

This week's *Torah* reading tells the dramatic story of the rebellion in the wilderness against the leadership of Moses by Korach and various other Israelites. The reading from the prophets that accompanies it, the *Haftarah*, is taken from the First Book of Samuel chapters 11 and 12. It tells of the anointing of King Saul and the warning by the prophet Samuel that Israel has to remain obedient to God, even though they now have a king as leader. Israel's covenant with God requires the creation of a society based on justice for everyone. Samuel is concerned that with the appointment of their first king he might abuse his power and undermine the values of the covenant. In both of the passages a leader of the nation, whether Moses or Samuel, invites a public scrutiny of his activities for any evidence that he has acted in a corrupt way or abused his power.

In the rebellion against Moses he is accused of failing as a political leader to bring the children of Israel into a land flowing with milk and honey as he had promised. The Bible records for the first time that Moses loses his temper!

> And Moses was greatly angry and said to the Eternal: 'Do not turn to their offering! Not one donkey of theirs did I take, nor did I harm any single one of them.' (Numbers 16.15)

Moses was making a public oath before God so as to demonstrate that he had been totally honest in his dealings. But why
illustrate his honesty by referring to never having taken a donkey? The rabbis suggested a solution. Moses had used his own
donkey when he travelled from Midian back to Egypt to confront
Pharaoh. He was so scrupulous in his behaviour that even
though he was entitled to ask the Israelites to refund him for the
food the donkey had eaten on the way and any other legitimate
expenses, he refused to ask for payment. He did not charge
mileage!

When Samuel handed over authority to King Saul he also
made a declaration before the people that he had never taken
advantage of his leadership position for his own private purposes. So this is one of the themes linking the two passages. Samuel
says:

> Here I am, testify against me before the Eternal and before
> his anointed: Whose ox have I taken? Or whose donkey have I
> taken? Whom have I defrauded? Whom have I oppressed?
> From whose hand have I taken a bribe to blind my eyes with
> it, so that I may restore it to you? (I Samuel 12.3)

The people confirm that Samuel is indeed guiltless of any such
crimes.

When Samuel asserts that he has always acted with integrity he
is also giving another hint to the people about the risks of
appointing a king. He had already warned them that a king
would confiscate their land and give it to his friends. He would
also take their young men and women, and even take their don-
keys to work for him (I Samuel 8.16). Samuel is stepping down
but demonstrating to the people and, indeed, to his successor
King Saul, that a true leader in Israel must act within the law and
behave with integrity.

Both of our passages show that leaders must be publicly
accountable, and that their activities, in particular their financial

transactions, must be utterly transparent and open to inspection.

Moses only referred to one specific wrongdoing, taking a donkey, whereas Samuel speaks of five separate situations that a leader might exploit for his own advantage. For Moses leading the Israelites through the wilderness the opportunities for abusing his power were relatively few so one example was enough. For Samuel, living amongst a settled community on the verge of becoming a nation, the temptations of office were far greater. How might we understand Samuel's list today?

An ox in biblical times was an expensive animal to own, so to steal someone's ox would have been a serious crime. But the rabbis understood the verse in another way. They pointed out that Samuel used to offer sacrifices of oxen to God and use the occasion to plead to God to show mercy on the people. So the rabbis suggested that whenever Samuel made such a sacrifice he did so using one of his own oxen and never asked the people to pay for it. That suggests that a leader should not be motivated primarily by the desire for personal gain, whether that meant financial reward or greater prestige, but should put the needs of the people he or she leads first. Leadership in this sense is a kind of personal sacrifice for the good of others.

The rabbis thought that Samuel, like Moses, used his own donkey when he travelled round the country on behalf of the people and never received payment, even though he was entitled to it. So this example would relate to all the perks of office that become available to political leaders. Using government transport for private travel, or making expense account purchases for what are really personal items, or hiring family or friends for special tasks, all such things are an abuse of the privileges of office. Samuel insists that his record in this area should also be properly examined.

The rabbis understood the third wrongdoing that Samuel mentions to mean 'defrauding' people. They meant when people take unfair advantage of a trust that has been given to them. A modern illustration would be the promises that politicians make before an election which they do not always fulfil once they are in power. Government is always more complicated than it might seem to those outside, so it is understandable if election promises have to be adjusted and compromises made. But promises that are given cynically just for the sake of being elected, with no intention of honouring them, are a breach of trust. Moreover, they bring the whole process of politics and government into disrepute. The rabbis call that kind of unacceptable behaviour, 'stealing the heart'.

Samuel's fourth question 'whom have I oppressed' is potentially even more serious. Leadership is often a delicate attempt to balance the needs and interests of a wide variety of groups within society. As one rabbi expressed it:

> Pray for the welfare of the government, for but for the fear it inspires, we would swallow each other alive! (Pirqe Avot 3.2)

But the temptation to any leader is to favour those who are most likely to re-elect him or her, to the neglect of others. In its mildest form this can lead to unfair treatment and discrimination. At its worst it can mean the deliberate isolation and even persecution of a particular minority. All too often leaders have stirred up the emotions of one sector of a society against another so as to further their own political ends or simply hold onto power. Samuel warns us that we must be aware of the particular biases or even prejudices of those we elect to positions of authority, and put in place the mechanisms which can monitor and correct any abuse of power.

The last element Samuel mentions, bribery, the selling of favours by those in power, is the most subversive and corrosive of crimes. For bribery destroys the judgment, and ultimately the reputation, of the one who accepts it, and corrupts the integrity of the one who gives it. Bribery undermines the basis of trust in the rule of law without which society cannot hold together.

If Moses and Samuel, amongst the greatest leaders of the biblical period, felt the need to place their record before the public for scrutiny, how much more so should anyone entrusted with a leadership role. No-one is above the temptations of power. It is our responsibility to ensure that safeguards are in place to prevent the kinds of abuse by leaders that Samuel describes and to encourage honest behaviour, for the sake of those in power as much as for ourselves. Unless we do so, we should not be surprised if our leaders fail us. For ultimately we have failed them.

FIGHTING FOR WOMEN'S RIGHTS

(*Pinchas* Numbers 25.10–30.11)

Our *parashah* this week contains the seeds of a revolution that never quite came to pass. Some of the ideas of this revolution have already had their effect on the teachings of the rabbis in the past. But it is only in the twentieth century that the truly radical nature of the issues that have to be addressed has been felt. We are in the middle of the revolution at this moment.

The issue is to be found in chapter 27 of the Book of Numbers. A problem was brought before Moses for a legal decision. It was so important, since it affected the nation as a whole, that the entire leadership of the people had to be assembled to hear the case – Elazar the high priest, the princes of the tribes, representing the traditional leadership of the people, and the '*edah*', the new representative assembly created by Moses.

The case was brought by five young women, sisters, all daughters of a man called Zelophehad the son of Hepher, son of Gilead, son of Machir, son of Manasseh from the tribe of Manasseh. These young women are considered so important in the biblical narrative that their names are given in full here and in other places. So let us honour them as well by naming them: Machlah, Noah, Choglah, Milkah and Tirzah.

The problem is as follows. According to the laws of inheritance throughout the Ancient Near East, it was not customary for women to inherit property. It would normally pass to the eldest son of the person who died, and in the absence of a son it would go to the nearest male relative. In this case Zelophehad had no sons, so the five daughters came to petition that they be allowed to inherit. This meant also that the name of their father would be preserved on the particular plot of land that was to be assigned to their family.

As part of their argument they pointed out that their father had not joined the rebellion against Moses led by Korach, so there was no reason why he might have forfeited his land – indeed his loyalty to Moses should be rewarded by the preservation of his name in this way.

Since the case was without precedent, and indeed cut to the heart of the assumptions that underlay the entire society, it required new legislation. Moses went to consult God.

God's response is unequivocal: The daughters of Zelophehad are right. You should certainly give them possession of an inheritance among their father's brothers and pass on to them their father's inheritance. This particular example of case law is to be enshrined in a new legal principle which is now spelled out:

> If a man dies and has no son, then his inheritance shall pass to his daughter. If he has no daughter then you shall give his inheritance to his brothers. If he has no brothers, then you shall give his inheritance to his father's brothers. And if his father has no brothers then you shall give his inheritance to the nearest family relative and he shall possess it. And this shall be a statute and ordinance, as the Eternal commanded Moses. (Numbers 27.8–11).

That should have been the end of the matter, but another problem was raised by the members of Zelophehad's tribe. Since the land of Israel is to be distributed between the various tribes so that each tribe has its own separate territory, this new law raises a problem. Suppose the daughters of Zelophehad marry someone from another tribe, then the inheritance will pass through their husbands, the male line, into the other tribe.

Moses replies again in the name of God:

> The tribe of the sons of Joseph are right! This is what the Eternal commands to the daughters of Zelophehad: Let them be wives to whoever is best in their eyes, *but* they must marry within the tribe of their father. The inheritance of the children of Israel shall not pass from one tribe to another for each man shall cleave to the inheritance of the tribe of his fathers. And every daughter who possesses an inheritance in any tribe of the people of Israel shall be a wife to one of the family of the tribe of her father so that everyone of the family of Israel may possess the inheritance of their fathers. (Numbers 36.5–8)

And that is how it worked in this particular case – the Bible records that the daughters of Zelophehad married sons of their father's brothers.

These two passages show something of the way biblical law works. The justice of both cases is shown: the daughters of Zelophehad should indeed inherit their father's property; on the other hand the other principle of the maintenance of the tribal divisions of the land must also be accepted. So a compromise is found that solves both problems.

But what the case shows very clearly is the fundamental assumption of Israelite society and the covenant itself – that the partner with God in the covenant is the autonomous adult Israelite male. Under normal circumstances it is the man who will inherit and the man who is the prime mover in legal matters. A woman's status is only clear and secure when she is either some man's daughter or some man's wife. The most vulnerable people in that society are widows and orphans – who do not fit into the covenant structure in their own right. That is why they are mentioned so often in the Bible as being in need of protection – by the society and by God. Where they have a limited standing in the law, they are dependent on the good will of others to support and protect them.

That is not to say that there was not social equality between men and women and indeed many outstanding women who acted as judges or prophets. But in a pattern that we are all too aware of today, the women who achieve such a high rank are seen as the exceptions. And indeed relatively little is known about the life of women either within the Bible or our own rabbinic tradition, because the writers are men writing about themselves within a formal structure of male dominance.

The challenge of the daughters of Zelophehad brought about one significant change of emphasis, but it was not enough to correct the bias of the structure of the covenant as a whole.

Today Zelophehad's daughters are once more being heard but now they do not come as petitioners dependent on male authority. The women's movement in the wider society has already had its impact on Jewish institutions and structures. We now take for granted that there are women rabbis working in America, and women graduates of the Leo Baeck College in London work in congregations in Britain and France. It has even been suggested that in this new century there will be women rabbis working in Orthodox congregations as well. If this seems to be a phenomenon of the last few decades only, it is worth remembering that the first woman rabbi in recent history was actually a product of German Jewry. Frau Rabbiner Regina Jonas was born in Berlin in 1902. She completed her studies at the *Lehranstalt für die Wissenschaft des Judentums* in 1930 and was given *semicha*, rabbinic ordination, by Rabbi Max Dienemann in 1934. She worked as a rabbi in Berlin, including giving regular sermons, until she was deported. She died in Auschwitz in 1944. Were it not for the *Shoah*, these major changes in our understanding of the place of women in Judaism might have begun over sixty years ago.

Where is the will of God to be found in this new challenge?

Some will claim that the tradition itself must be the final authority, the word of God revealed at Sinai and interpreted by the rabbinic authorities. But our *parashah* reminds us that Moses was willing to ask the difficult question of God on behalf of the daughters of Zelophehad, even though it meant going against every legal tradition and conventional assumption of his society. God's answer was to support the justice of their case, to overturn tradition in the name of truth.

Today the daughters of Zelophehad, Machlah, Noah, Choglah, Milkah and Tirzah, bring a whole new range of questions and of gifts to the leadership of the Jewish people. The revolution has begun and it offers us enormous possibilities for healing and renewal.

PROMISES! PROMISES!

(*Mattot-Mas'ei* Numbers 30.2–36.13)

Our *parashah* this *Shabbat* is a double one, *mattot-mas'ei*. It begins in Numbers chapter 30 with a commandment about someone who makes a vow, a *neder*, to God. In the biblical period it was a common practice to make vows to God. At a time of trouble someone would ask God for help and promise that if his prayers were answered, he would bring a special thanksgiving sacrifice to the temple. Or someone might vow to fast for a certain period as a special commitment to God. Our *parashah* goes on to point out a different set of conditions that applied to women because of the nature of Israelite society. While a man was considered to be totally responsible for what he vowed, a woman was not seen as an independent agent. If she was still living at home, her father had the authority to annul a vow that she had made, and if she was married, her husband had the same power over her. The Bible here reflects the values of its time, yet it also records one of the most moving of vows that was made by a woman. Hannah, a woman who was childless, promised that if she had a son she would dedicate him to God. When her son Samuel was born she took him to live in the temple at Shiloh and from then on was only able to see him during her annual visit. Hers was the conflict of a woman who longed for a child but was also deeply aware of her religious duty. Her vow made to God in the temple itself could not be set aside.

Part of Hannah's vow was that when her child grew up his hair would not be cut. This was a common practice when a man promised to dedicate himself to God for a particular period of time. Such a man became a *nazir*, and in addition to not cutting his hair, he would not drink wine or strong drink for the same period of time. He would have a status something like that of a priest and would have to avoid all kinds of ritual impurity at well. At the end of the period of his vow he would bring a special offering to the Temple and afterwards return to his normal life.

This practice of dedicating a special period of one's life to God as a *nazir* continued into rabbinic times and there is even a rabbinic story about a *nazir* that is very similar to the Greek legend about Narcissus. One young man became a *nazir* and grew his hair long but happened to catch a glimpse of his face reflected in a pool of water. He fell completely in love with the face that he saw there and was so affected that he had to go to a rabbi to get his vow annulled so that he could cut his hair and break the spell of this infatuation and return to normal life.

Such extreme kinds of vows are no longer part of Jewish life. But there is an echo of the practice of making a vow before God in some traditional synagogue services when someone promises to give money for the honour of being called to the *Torah* or of having another *mitzvah* during the service. Since the money cannot be paid on the spot if it is a *Shabbat* or Festival, this can only be a vow that the man promises to pay later. To make such a vow is called 'to *schnodder*' and it comes from our word *neder*, a vow. The Hebrew phrase *mi shennadar*, 'the one who made a *neder*, a vow', simply becomes shortened in Yiddish to *schnodder*.

While the Bible seems to accept that people would often make such vows, it is not altogether happy about this. After all, it is one thing to promise something to God, but what if you could not fulfil it in the end. Why get yourself into trouble? The rabbis gave the example of people who promise to give to charity in the enthusiasm of the moment but come to regret it later and try to escape from their promise when the collector comes round. The problem is already pointed out in the Book of Ecclesiastes:

> When you make a promise to God, do not delay in fulfilling it, for God has no pleasure in fools! Whatever you vow fulfil. … Let not your mouth cause guilt to your body and plead before the collector 'it was just a mistake'! (Ecclesiastes 5.3,5)

When they discussed this passage the rabbis added all the excuses that people came up with in their day to avoid paying their charity pledges. They said:

> This refers to someone who made a public pledge to charity and then refused to pay. Do not tell the charity collector when he comes: 'I did not really mean what I said. My pledge was not meant to be taken seriously. I only spoke out in order to avoid public embarrassment or so that others may pledge, but I did not, and I do not intend to give any of my own money.' Or perhaps he will say: 'I did not know what I was doing.' Or: 'At the time I made the pledge I was confident I would be able to pay but now I find I cannot.'

None of these excuses, said the rabbis, will be acceptable to God. One of the rabbis concluded that it was better not to make promises of that sort at all just in case you could not fulfil them in the end.

The most familiar use of the word *neder* is in the evening service for Yom Kippur, the *Kol Nidre*. In that service we recite an ancient formula that absolves us of all vows that we make to God from one year to the next. In the Middle Ages the *Kol Nidre* prayer became something of an embarrassment at times to the Jewish community. Those who wished to attack the Jews said that the words meant that you could not do business with a Jew because once a year he would simply annul all the vows that he had made! Now it is quite clear from the biblical text, and from the *Kol Nidre* itself, that what was intended here was not business agreements or contracts or indeed any vows made with other people. Instead the vows mentioned here are those made to God alone.

Here we find an echo of the biblical vows that are mentioned in our *parashah*, but the idea is still relevant for us today. At the time of the New Year, we look for a fresh beginning to our lives. During the Ten Days of Penitence we attempt to resolve and remove conflicts that we have with other people, because only when we have obtained forgiveness from them can we ask forgiveness from God. But there are all kinds of mistakes and failures in our lives that we need to examine – promises we made that we somehow never kept, times when we were less than honest with ourselves. It is these matters between us and God that are also addressed by the *Kol Nidre* service. So it gives us an opportunity to admit that we do not always live up to what we could be, to acknowledge our weaknesses and failures, to admit that we may not always be right and that we also share responsibility for the conflicts that we have with others.

Though we do not make vows in the biblical sense, our promises do have consequences for ourselves and others. If the words we say cannot be trusted, our whole society begins to fall apart. As the rabbis said: 'Let your yes be a yes, and your no a no.' In this sense, every word we utter is a *neder*, a vow we personally make to God.

THE ONE AND THE MANY

(*Ekev* Deuteronomy 7.12–11.25)

Towards the end of this week's *Torah* reading (Deuteronomy 11.13–21) comes a passage that is very familiar to anyone who prays in a Jewish service on a regular basis. It is known in the Jewish liturgy as the 'second paragraph of the *Shema*' and is usually read silently by the community.

The reason it is included in the service is because of some of the words that it contains which are identical with those in the *Shema* itself. Both passages say that we should talk about the teachings of God, 'when you lie down and when you rise up'. This is understood to mean that we should recite in the morning and evening services the *Shema* itself, the prayer that begins 'Hear O Israel, the Eternal our God, the Eternal is One.'

But this particular paragraph has another dimension as well. Jewish tradition teaches us that when we recite the first paragraph of the *Shema*, we take upon ourselves the *ol malchut shamayim*, the 'yoke of the kingdom of heaven'. That is to say we accept that our lives are given over to the service of God. By reciting the second paragraph, we are said to submit ourselves to the *ol ha-mitzvot*, the 'yoke of the commandments', we accept the commandments of God as binding upon ourselves.

Nevertheless there are problems with the paragraph itself. It says, in effect, if you obey My commandments I will bring the rain to the land and everything will go well. But if you do not obey then I will withhold the rain, the land will not give up its produce and you will perish swiftly from off the good land I have given you.

It is a very tidy theology. Obedience to God brings reward, disobedience brings punishment. It assumes a system that works mechanically and efficiently. But the reality of human experience is nothing like this. In fact much of the Hebrew Bible is asking questions about this very problem: why is it that good people are not always rewarded? In fact they may suffer tragically in their lives. Conversely there are many bad people walking about on the earth who seem to live charmed lives, certainly no divine punishment falls upon them. The prophet Jeremiah challenges God on this score. Some of the Psalms ask pointed questions about the same problem. The entire Book of Job is a refutation of this kind of simple reward-and-punishment view of the universe. None of them comes to a fully satisfactory solution. Job concludes that the workings of God are greater and more mysterious than we can fathom. God can be challenged, must be challenged, but our final response can only be resignation and humility. This may be the answer for some but when faced with events of the magnitude of the *Shoah*, even such deeply felt answers feel inadequate.

But is our text in Deuteronomy really as simplistic as it appears at first glance? There is one oddity about the text that needs to be looked at. Most of the passage is expressed in the plural form – Israel as a whole is addressed. However from time to time the verbs change into the singular form. The individual is addressed.

Our section begins in the plural, for the whole of Israel is being spoken to.

> If you will surely listen to My commandments which I command you this day, to love the Eternal your God and to serve God with all your heart and with all your soul, then I shall give the rain of your land in its season, the former and the latter rain … (Deuteronomy 11.13–14a)

At this point the person being addressed becomes the single individual.

> And thou shalt gather thy grain and thy wine and thy oil. And I will give grass in thy fields for thy cattle, and thou shalt eat and be full. (Deuteronomy 11.14b–15)

If all of Israel is obedient to the will of God then blessings will be given to every single household. But immediately after this the text switches back to the plural form again. This is the part which includes the warnings that disobedience to God will lead to the rain being withheld and the land not yielding its fruit so that the people is destroyed. It should be pointed out that the commands we are to obey include those about caring for the land itself, for example, letting it lie fallow every seven years and not destroying trees. So there is also an ecological basis to this warning.

Our text now returns to the positive command to make God's words a central part of our lives. We are still in the plural, at least for the opening words:

> You shall put these words upon your heart and upon your soul and you shall bind them as a sign upon your hands and they shall be as frontlets between your eyes, and you shall teach them to your children to speak of them ... (Deuteronomy 11.18–19a)

At this point once again the text returns to the singular form, and in fact picks up the exact version that is so familiar from the first paragraph of the *Shema*.

> ... when thou sittest in thine house and when thou walkest by the way and when thou liest down and when thou risest up, and thou shalt write them as a sign upon the doorposts of thy house and at thy gates. (Deuteronomy 11.19b–20).

What is the purpose of this change of language? It may simply be a wish to repeat the exact same words in the same form as

appeared earlier in the *Shema* paragraph so that they become
more deeply embedded in our hearts and minds. Perhaps it is
also to reinforce the idea that these general principles are to
apply to each and every individual. It is you who is meant, you
who are to teach your own children, to speak of these things in
your own personal home, and to keep a tangible sign of them on
your own personal doorpost.

But perhaps it is also a way of acknowledging that our
individual fate is not so easily described or explained. If all of
Israel does wrong or right, then maybe we can literally affect the
climate, change the seasons to bring rain or prevent it. But even
if it were possible to measure the good or bad of a society in such
terms, our own individual story cannot simply be fitted into
some such general pattern. We can be the victims of the failings
of our society – but we each contribute to the forces that make
that society what it is. Our passage does make a general statement
about reward and punishment, but recognizes the reality of our
individual fate and our individual choice.

The story is told of a young man who went away from his
home to undertake Jewish studies for seven years. When he
returned his father asked him what he had learned. He answered,
'I learned that you should love your neighbour as yourself.' 'You
needed seven years to learn that?' exclaimed his father. 'Everyone
knows that. You even knew it before you went away!' 'Yes,' said
his son, 'but now I know that it means that *I* should love my
neighbour as myself.'

UNDERSTANDING ISAIAH

(*Re'eh, Haftarah* Isaiah 54.11–55.5)

I have very ambivalent feelings about this week's *Torah* reading. It was the portion that was read on the *Shabbat* when I was *Barmitzvah* and my father taught me how to chant the *Haftarah*, the prophetic reading. While other boys in my Orthodox synagogue learnt how to read from the *Torah* scroll for their *Barmitzvah* as well, I did not. I was a very shy boy and not very self-confident, and would burst into tears under stress. So my religion school teachers and my parents decided that it was much safer if I did not do too much public reading. 'Besides,' said my father, 'you will never again be called upon to read from the scroll when you grow up, but you might well be asked to chant the *Haftarah* in synagogue so you should know it.'

So a part of me is fond of today's prophetic reading from Isaiah 54 since I can still chant it with my father's special melody. But when I remember how difficult it was having to learn it, and how much of an ordeal my Barmitzvah was, I stop being so sentimental. When I see how well prepared and comfortable my son was with his Barmitzvah and my daughter with her Bat-mitzvah in our Reform Synagogue in London I am rather jealous of them.

Although I managed to chant the *Haftarah* passage successfully in the synagogue on the day itself, I had no understanding whatsoever of what I was reading. Of course some prophetic readings are more difficult than others but just looking at the opening words of the *Haftarah* today is a reminder of how obscure they can be.

> 'O afflicted one, storm-tossed, and not comforted, behold, I will set your stones in antimony, and lay your foundations with sapphires. I will make your pinnacles of agate, your gates of carbuncles and your wall of precious stones.' (Isaiah 54.11–12)

Today I know that 'the afflicted one' in this poetic text refers to Jerusalem. The passage is a word of comfort to the people of Israel living in exile in Babylon and the prophet is promising them that they will soon return to their land and rebuild Jerusalem. I also know that this passage was chosen to be read at this time of the year for a special reason. A few weeks ago we experienced the black fast of *Tisha B'Av*, the ninth day of the month of *Av*, when we remember the destruction of the Temple and Jerusalem. All the prophetic readings since *Tisha B'Av* are meant to bring comfort and consolation. They are the promises of restoration, of the ingathering of the exiles to the promised land and rebuilding, that will accompany us over the summer months till the time of the Jewish New Year. All of this I know now, but it made no sense to me when I was thirteen years old, and I had to train as a rabbi in order to understand it!

So what is one supposed to make of such passages? There is an argument that even though the verses are obscure and we do not understand a word, they are part of Jewish tradition and it is enough to recite them because that is what we are supposed to do. It is simply our duty and that is the end of the matter. A variation on this argument is to say that it is enough to let the beauty of the sounds they make and the melody of the chanting flow over us like a mantra – after all if the sounds are comforting they will have achieved their purpose. But that cannot be enough. The words of the prophet were not obscure when he first spoke them or else they would have been of no use to the people suffering in exile who heard them. And if they had no meaning they would certainly not have been carefully preserved for over 2000 years. The rabbis must also have had some understanding of them when they chose to read them each year in the synagogue at this time. In fact Judaism insists that we should try to understand what we read. We recite three times each day the blessing that says:

> You grace human beings with knowledge and teach mortals insight; grace us with the knowledge, insight and understanding that come from You. Blessed are You, Eternal, who graces us with knowledge.

Understanding, intelligence and discernment are the gifts we receive and request from God as human beings. However difficult the text may be it is our task to try to understand it, to wrestle with its many levels of meaning and ultimately to hear behind it the voice of God speaking to us.

In fact our *Haftarah* is most explicit about this idea. The next verse says:

> 'All your sons shall be taught by the Eternal, and great shall be the peace of your sons.' (Isaiah 54.13)

What greater text could there be for a *Barmitzvah* or *Batmitzvah* to read. It calls us to study the word of God and through this study to bring about peace.

Perhaps with this promise of the prophet in mind we can read the opening words again and try to understand their imagery. Jerusalem will be rebuilt, the prophet promises. But not with walls made of the usual stone. For stone walls are designed to keep people out, to turn Jerusalem into a fortress, a defence against attack. In the vision of the prophet when Jerusalem is rebuilt it will be constructed with precious stones. Its very walls will radiate light and colour, they will dazzle with their beauty and draw people near to experience their radiance. It is the

Jerusalem of dreams and hopes that the prophet sees in the future, not the city of war and conflict. It is a vision that is still before us however distant it seems, however hard the journey to reach it.

The prophet understood this as well. The physical Jerusalem is a place that people wish to possess, to own for themselves, so it will always be a place of conflict. The Jerusalem of vision is a place of justice, where conflicts are resolved without violence or terror, where all can find a home because the true and only owner is God. As the prophet says:

> In righteousness you shall be established; you shall be far from oppression, for you shall not fear; and from terror, for it shall not come near you. (Isaiah 54.14)

May these words come true in our lifetime and in our days.

PREPARING FOR A NEW YEAR

(*Ha-chodesh* Isaiah 66)

This *Shabbat* is different from the regular pattern of readings from the Pentateuch and Prophets. We choose a special prophetic text because this *Shabbat* coincides with the appearance in the sky of a new moon and hence a new month in the Jewish calendar. The prophetic reading comes from the Book of Isaiah chapter 66, and the last verse but one of the chapter mentions the new moon as a special time.

> And it shall come to pass that from one new moon to another and from one *Shabbat* to another that all flesh shall come to worship before Me, says the Eternal. (v. 23)

The particular idea that 'all flesh shall come to worship before God' takes on added significance in the month ahead of us. It is called *Elul* and it marks the beginning of the great penitential season that accompanies the Jewish New Year. Since Jewish tradition sees the first day of the New Year as the actual birthday of the world, we understand this season as having significance not just for the Jewish people but for the whole world.

From tomorrow, Sunday, in synagogues throughout the world, Jews will be blowing the *shofar*, the ram's horn, as a way of awakening us to this special penitential season. The *shofar* calls us to review our lives, to examine our actions during the past year, to try to make amends for any wrong that we have done, to repent of all the failures that we can see and to seek forgiveness from each other and then from God.

It is an extraordinary period of time for the Jewish community. The imagery is quite vivid. On the New Year's Day, *Rosh Hashanah*, God opens up the Book of Life in which every person's story is written. In this view it is like a bookkeeping ledger in which all the good things and all the bad things that a person has done during the past year are recorded. But it is important to note that this is no mechanical business as has sometimes been suggested. The rabbis taught that those who are completely bad are written down for death in the year ahead and those who are completely good are written down for life. But they added that only God knows how the balance is, and anyway, most of us fall somewhere inbetween, neither wholly bad nor wholly good. So we are given the opportunity during the next ten days to try to set the record straight; to examine our lives, as it were, through God's eyes. We are required to try to see the things we have done wrong, to look seriously at the actions we feel guilty about and acknowledge our failure to offer sufficient help to others. We are to do a *cheshbon hanefesh*, a personal accounting of our souls, to admit to ourselves our failures, our stupidities, our greeds; the damage we inflicted on others; the ways we cheated in our dealings with the world; the cries for help to which we did not respond; the religious study and duties that we failed to do.

But regret and feeling sorry are not considered to be enough. We must take active steps to compensate for the harm we have done, make up our relationships that have been damaged in the past year, and if we have done any real wrongdoing, take the necessary steps to correct it.

On the tenth day of the New Year, the Day of Atonement, we stand as a community before God when the judgment is made and the Book of our lives is closed and sealed. If we have done our work of repentance and repair well, then God will forgive us. We cannot cancel out the past or remove it. The things we have done continue to have consequences in our own life and in the life of others. But our actions can undo some of the damage, and if our repentance has been sincere it will have affected how we respond on future occasions when we are tempted to act in the wrong way. In fact that is the measure of the sincerity and genuineness of our repentance – some tangible change in our behaviour. And if, but only if, we do our work, we can safely leave it to God to tidy up the rest of the mess we have created. God 'covers over it', which is the meaning of the Hebrew verb *kapar*, which we translate as 'atonement', *Yom Kippur*, 'the Day of Atonement'.

But we must be clear about the dynamics of this process. The rabbis said that the Day of Atonement atones for sins between human beings and God – but it does not atone for sins that people do to each other until they have first gone through all the phases of repentance and repair and reconciliation that I have described. God's personal honour is easily satisfied. What offends God is our mistreatment of fellow human beings, because we are all made in the image of God.

Since the Jewish New Year is understood as being the birthday of the entire world, our tradition teaches that not just the Jewish people are examined and tested during this period, but all peoples and all creatures. As the passage from our *Haftarah* said, 'all flesh shall come to worship before Me'. So some of the principles of this High Holyday period may also be of value to others.

Firstly, we may recognize that no change for the better can happen without a proper examination of our past and an acknowledgment of the things that have made us what we are – the good and bad actions and experiences that have helped shape our life. We are their product and as long as we do not acknowledge those past events that to some extent continue to control us, we have no freedom and we are doomed to repeat our follies and destructive actions, whether as individuals or even as nations.

Secondly, we may learn that to change our patterns of behaviour we need to replace them with others, beginning with a recognition that an overwhelming concern with our past guilt can itself become self-destructive. The chasidic master Yitzhak Meir of Ger said:

> People who talk about and think about the evil they have done, are thinking evil, and are caught up in what they are thinking about. Stir filth this way or that, and it is still filth ... In the time I brood I could be stringing pearls for the joy of heaven. You have done wrong? Then balance it by doing right!

Thirdly, we can take some comfort in the knowledge that not everything is in our control, that there are things we can and must leave to God. This is not a licence for complacency, because we must have done all the work on ourselves that we can. But we ourselves are not God. We are not the ultimate arbiters of reality and we should not think of ourselves as so important that nothing can happen without us, or imagine that we must be in total control of our lives and of the lives of those around us. But neither should we imagine ourselves as being so small and insignificant that nothing that we do matters and that we have no authority or responsibility in the world. We are each unique and accountable before God – and each of us is special and loved by God for who and what we are.

Though one might expect that this penitential season is only solemn and formal, it has a certain inner joy, because it gives us a chance to take ourselves seriously and explore for a limited time the deeper meaning of our life. We can shut out the background noises of the day, the routines and conventions that fill up our time and try to go beyond the superficiality of so many of our actions and our relationships for most of the rest of the year. We can find space and time for our souls. In the words of the great nineteenth-century rabbi and teacher Samson Raphael Hirsch:

> The sound of the *shofar* calls us to God. It calls poor and rich to true riches; it calls the most distant wanderer home.

ACCOUNTABILITY

(*Ki Tavo* Deuteronomy 26.1–29.8)

We are currently in the period of preparation for the Jewish New Year, *Rosh Hashanah*, which is known as *Yom Ha-Din*, the Day of Judgment on our individual lives and on the life of our Jewish community. So as we read this week's passage from the *Torah*, we will be looking for something that addresses this season.

The reading for this *Shabbat* offers a good example of how a few extra words in a biblical sentence have opened the way to some important ideas. At the beginning of our reading from Deuteronomy 26, the Israelites are instructed to take some of the first fruit of the harvest and bring it to a central place of worship in the land of Israel and give it to the priest. But the sentence adds the phrase: to the priest 'who shall be in those days'. The common sense meaning of these extra words is quite simple. The speaker is Moses and he is looking forward to a future time when the Israelites will have entered the promised land. The Israelites are to bring the fruit to the priest who will be there at that time in the future.

But since it is common sense that you can only bring the fruit to the priest who is there at the time, the phrase 'who shall be in those days' seems to be superfluous. The door is now open to looking for a deeper interpretation of these extra words. The same extra phrase has already appeared in an earlier verse in the Book of Deuteronomy, chapter 17 verse 9. This passage concerns a legal procedure and the text says:

> You shall come to the levitical priests and to the judge who
> shall be in those days and ask, and they shall tell you the words
> of judgment.

Again the question arises – to what judge can you go except the
one who will be there 'in those days'?

The rabbinic explanation is powerful and has considerable
consequences. They understood it as follows: even though the
judge in your own days is not like the judges that have been there
in previous times, you have to accept the judgment he gives
because he is the competent person in your time and place
(Babylonian Talmud, Rosh Hashanah 25b). To illustrate their
point, the rabbis compare the judge Jephthah, whose story is told
in the Book of Judges, with the great judge and prophet Samuel.
Jephthah was a successful military leader but he so wanted to win
a particular battle that he vowed to sacrifice to God the first creature to come and greet him on his successful return. It happened
to be his daughter who came out and Jephthah kept his vow.
Clearly Jephthah is not the best example of how a judge should
behave! Nevertheless the rabbis made the point that 'Jephthah in
his generation was equivalent to Samuel in his generation.' In
one sense it may mean that each generation gets the leadership it
deserves! But it points to the need to accept and respect the
authority of those you place in leadership positions in your own
time.

The problem is that this attitude is contradicted by an equally
strong tendency in Judaism to assert that the leaders of previous
generations were far greater than we could ever be in our generation. So how could we presume to offer our own opinions if they
differ from those of the past. Who are we to dare to change what
they have decided in their greater wisdom?! Such respect for the
past must have its proper place, but it may also paralyse our own
creativity and our ability to address new situations.

The passage we just read referred to judges, the legal and

political authorities of the time. But our passage this week speaks about the priest who shall be 'in those days', the spiritual leader of the Israelite community. So in matters of contemporary religious issues we also have to recognize the authority of the spiritual leaders we appoint in our own times. New times, new circumstances may need new religious answers, even if they contradict those that we venerate from the past.

So should we simply preserve the traditions inherited from past leaders or should we follow instead the innovations of the leaders of today? The answer, of course, is that either option can be followed depending on the circumstances. But who is to decide which line to follow at any given time?

The answer to this question also lies in the texts we have read, for there is a third party present in both of them – the people to whom Moses is speaking. We are the ones who are spoken to; we are the ones who are to go to the judge or priest of our own days, because we are the ones who give them authority to decide on our behalf. So these texts contain another kind of challenge. We also have to take full responsibility for the election of our leadership, political and religious. But our responsibility does not stop there. We have to ensure that they are publicly accountable for their actions. Everything we give into the hands of our leadership must be open to inspection and made transparent – from financial matters to decisions of religious practice. A Jewish community that does not take such responsibility for its appointed representatives and functionaries invites corruption. If we do not monitor their actions and question their decisions, we are unfair to them as well, because we open the door to temptation, whether it be financial misuse or the abuse of the power they have over others. On *Rosh Hashanah* we are held responsible for the things that they do in our name. We too have to face a judgment.

May we take this responsibility seriously so that we can always go with confidence and trust to the priests and judges, to the appointed leaders of our Jewish community 'who shall be in those days'.

REPENTANCE

(*Shabbat Shuvah*)

This is a strange week in the Jewish calendar. It is a kind of limbo period, suspended between two days of enormous religious power: *Rosh Hashanah*, the first day of the New Year, and *Yom Kippur*, the Day of Atonement.

Rosh Hashanah has a variety of names which reflect the different ideas to be found within it.

Jewish tradition has understood it to be the anniversary of the creation of the world. As one of the mediaeval liturgical hymns expresses it: *ha-yom harat olam*. 'This day is the birthday of the world.' But the day is not marked by a birthday party or a celebration. Instead it is seen as a day of judgment when all of creation passes in review before God. Has it fulfilled the hopes and expectations of its creator? This question applies to all of nature as well as human beings. According to the tradition even the angels who have no role other than to do the will of God tremble on this day, for as another liturgical poem says: 'judgment comes upon the hosts of heaven'.

According to this tradition our deeds of the past year are examined and a judgment is formed on our lives – are we to live out the coming year or not? And just in case we forget how random life and death must seem from a human perspective a liturgical poem spells this out in precise detail:

who will live and who will die, who at the full span of their lives and who not, who will die by fire and who by water, who by human violence and who by the violence of beasts, who by hunger and who by thirst, who by disaster, plague or execution, who will rest and who will wander, who will be secure and who tormented, who will become poor and who rich, who will fail and who succeed.

It is so explicit that it is no wonder that reforming Jewish movements of the nineteenth century cut it from the liturgy. Yet the poem has been re-introduced by some Reform and Liberal Jewish liturgies today. We are a tougher generation after the horrors of the twentieth century. We expect a liturgy that confronts us with reality and does not hide it from us.

Others objected that the prayer is fatalistic, as if our destiny is sealed on that one day and nothing we do can change it. But the fact remains that we do not know what our fate will be in the coming year, or even the next moment. The same prayer goes on to tell us that 'penitence, prayer and charity' can indeed change our destiny. Of course we cannot know what might have happened had we acted differently. Only God knows. But performing acts of 'penitence, prayer and charity' will certainly change *us*, so that we are better prepared to face whatever confronts us in the coming year

The New Year's day has a further title – *Yom Ha-Zikkaron*, the Day of Remembering. Again it fits the theme of judgment. We are to remember the wrong deeds we have committed during the past year and try to correct things, and restore our relationship with anyone we have harmed. But this name for the day indicates that God also remembers. Indeed the rabbis taught that it is better for us to remember and take responsibility for our past. For whatever we prefer to forget, God is certain to remember for us, and bring us to judgment.

If all this sounds very negative, we must not forget that awaiting us, ten days later, is *Yom Kippur*. Though seemingly a grim

day of fasting and serious prayer, it is actually a celebration and
a great opportunity. It is a celebration because of its theme of the
possibility of reconciliation with God. It assumes the possibility
of human change, of spiritual growth and development. Though
we can have no prior knowledge of our particular fate, we are
free to try to change our lives, to learn from past mistakes so
that we do not have to repeat them endlessly. *Yom Kippur* is an
affirmation that life is not predetermined, that we are not
puppets but rather responsible actors in the drama that is our
personal story.

Yom Kippur offers us the special gift of a day outside of time.
Because we neither eat nor drink, our natural functions do not
intrude. We have the luxury of standing back from our lives, as
if detached from their daily pressures. We have the opportunity
to meditate about who we are, where we are in our lives, what are
our real priorities, what are our values. We can think about
family and friends and what needs to be done to improve our
relationships. Indeed we can explore a thousand and one private
issues it is otherwise difficult to confront. *Yom Kippur* offers a
space for that precious perspective that comes when we try to
imagine how our lives must look when seen through God's eyes
– detached, compassionate and caring about where we have
come from and where we are going to.

But on this *Shabbat* we are somewhere inbetween. *Rosh
Hashanah*, the Day of Judgment when the book detailing our life
was opened lies behind us. Before us is *Yom Kippur*, the great day
of contemplation and reconciliation. So this *Shabbat* is aptly
called *shabbat shuvah*, literally the 'sabbath of turning'. The verb
shuv, which means 'to turn', to turn away, to turn back, to turn
around, suggests the many dimensions of *teshuvah*, 'repentance'.
We can turn back to review our past; we try to turn away from
mistaken ways and attitudes, from false values and priorities; and
we turn or return to God in whatever way we understand that
power to which we are ultimately answerable; and finally we turn

towards the future, to the promise and hope of *Yom Kippur* and an unknown lifetime beyond it.

Another part of the liturgy for these days provides an exquisite poem on the transience of life. It offers little comfort, but it gives a true perspective. For what is really important and what is trivial in our life? What will survive us and what will disappear when we go? These are the kind of questions that haunt us at this solemn moment in our religious year. As the poem reminds us:

> We come from the dust and end in dust. We spend our life earning our living, but we are fragile like a cup so easily broken, like grass that withers, like flowers that fade, like passing shadows and dissolving clouds, a fleeting breeze and dust that scatters, like a dream that fades away.

On this *Shabbat*, in this time-in-between, we prepare ourselves to face this truth about our limited existence, and then go on to celebrate once again the renewed life we have been given.

APPENDICES

APPENDIX 1

THE *TORAH* AND *HAFTARAH* READINGS

Parashah	Bible text	Haftarah (Ashkenazi)
	THE BOOK OF GENESIS	
Bereshit	Genesis 1.1–6.8	Isaiah 42.5–43.10
Noach	Genesis 6.9–11.32	Isaiah 54.1–55.5
Lech Lecha	Genesis 12.1–17.27	Isaiah 40.27–41.16
Vayera	Genesis 18.1–22.24	II Kings 6.1–37
Chayei Sarah	Genesis 23.1–25.18	I Kings 1.1–31
Toledoth	Genesis 25.19–28.9	Malachi 1.1–2.7
Vayyetze	Genesis 28.10–32.3	Hosea 12.13–14.10
Vayyishlach	Genesis 32.4–36.43	Hosea 11.7–12.12
Vayyeshev	Genesis 37.1–40.23	Amos 2.6–3.8
Mikketz	Genesis 41.1–44.17	I Kings 3.15–4.1
Vayyiggash	Genesis 44.18–47.27	Ezekiel 37.15–28
Vayyechi	Genesis 47.28–50.26	I Kings 2.1–12
	THE BOOK OF EXODUS	
Shemoth	Exodus 1.1–6.1	Isaiah 27.6–28.13; 29.22–23
Va'era	Exodus 6.2–9.35	Ezekiel 28.25–29.21
Bo	Exodus 10.1–13.16	Jeremiah 46.13–28
Beshallach	Exodus 13.27–17.16	Judges 4.4–5.31
Yitro	Exodus 18.1–20.23	Isaiah 6.1–7.6; 9.5–6
Mishpatim	Exodus 21.1–24.18	Jeremiah 34.8–22; 33.25–26
Terumah	Exodus 25.1–27.19	I Kings 5.26–6.13
Tetzaveh	Exodus 27.20–30.10	Ezekiel 43.10–27

Ki Tissa	Exodus 30.11–34.35	I Kings 18.1–39
Vayyakhel	Exodus 35.1–38.20	I Kings 7.40–50
Pekudei	Exodus 38.21–40.38	I Kings 7.51–8.21

THE BOOK OF LEVITICUS

Vayyikra	Leviticus 1.1–5.26	Isaiah 43.21–44.23
Tzav	Leviticus 6.1–8.36	Jeremiah 7.21–8.3; 9.22–23
Shemini	Leviticus 9.1–11.47	II Samuel 6.1–7.17
Tazria	Leviticus 12.1–13.59	II Kings 4.42–5.19
Metzora	Leviticus 14.1–15.33	II Kings 7.3–20
Acharei Mot	Leviticus 16.1–18.30	Ezekiel 22.1–19
Kedoshim	Leviticus 19.1–20.27	Amos 9.7–15
Emor	Leviticus 21.1–24.23	Ezekiel 44.15–31
Behar	Leviticus 25.1–26.2	Jeremiah 32.6–27
B'chukotai	Leviticus 26.3–27.34	Jeremiah 16.19–17.14

THE BOOK OF NUMBERS

Bemidbar	Numbers 1.1–4.20	Hosea 2.1–22
Naso	Numbers 4.21–7.89	Judges 8.2–25
B'ha'alotecha	Numbers 8.1–12.16	Zechariah 2.14–4.7
Shelach Lecha	Numbers 13.1–15.41	Joshua 2.1–24
Korach	Numbers 16.1–18.32	I Samuel 11.14–12.22
Chukkat	Numbers 19.1–22.1	Judges 11.1–33
Balak	Numbers 22.2–25.9	Micah 5.6–6.8
Pinchas	Numbers 25.10–30.1	I Kings 18.46–19.21
Mattot	Numbers 30.2–32.42	Jeremiah 1.1–2.3
Mass'ei	Numbers 33.1–36.13	Jeremiah 2.4–28; 3.4; 4.1–2

THE BOOK OF DEUTERONOMY

Devarim	Deuteronomy 1.1–3.22	Isaiah 1.1–27
Va-etchanan	Deuteronomy 3.23–7.11	Isaiah 40.1–26
Ekev	Deuteronomy 7.12–11.25	Isaiah 49.14–51.3
Re'eh	Deuteronomy 11.26–16.17	Isaiah 54.11–55.5
Shofetim	Deuteronomy 16.18–21.9	Isaiah 51.12–52.12
Ki Tetze	Deuteronomy 21.10–25.19	Isaiah 54.1–10
Ki Tavo	Deuteronomy 26.1–29.8	Isaiah 60.1–22
Nitzavim	Deuteronomy 29.9–30.20	Isaiah 61.10–63.9

Vayyelech	Deuteronomy 31.1–30	Hosea 14.2–10; Micah 7.18–20; Joel 2.15–27
Ha'azinu	Deuteronomy 32.1–52	II Samuel 22.1–51
Vezot Ha'berachah	Deuteronomy 33.1–34.12	Joshua 1.1–18

(The *Haftarot* listed here follow the Ashkenazi tradition)

APPENDIX 2

THE JEWISH MONTHS

Tishri (September/October)

1 New Year First Day
2 New Year Second Day
3 Fast of Gedaliah
10 Day of Atonement
15 Succot First Day
16 Succot Second Day
17–21 Hol Ha-moed
    (Intermediate days)
21 Hoshanah Rabbah
22 Eighth Day festival
23 Simchat Torah

Marcheshvan (October/November)
Kislev (November/December)   25 Chanukkah
Tevet (December)   10 Fast of Tevet
Shevat (December/January)   15 New Year for Trees
Adar (January/February)   13 Fast of Esther
      14 Purim

Nissan (March/April)   14 Eve of Passover
      15 Passover First Day
      16 Passover Second Day
      17–20 Hol Ha-moed
          (Intermediate days)
      21 Passover Seventh Day
      22 Passover Eighth Day
      27 Yom Ha-Shoah

Iyyar (April/May)

5 Israel Independence
  Day
18 Lag Ba-omer (33rd
  Day of the Omer)

Sivan (May/June

6 Shavuot First Day
7 Shavuot Second Day

Tammuz (June/July)

17 Fast of Tammuz

Av (July/August)

9 Fast of Av

Elul (August/September)

The Jewish calendar is lunisolar: the months are calculated according to the moon, and the years according to the sun. Since there are eleven days left over after each twelve months, an additional month (a second month of Adar) is added in each seven out of every nineteen years to ensure that the annual cycle of festivals keep their original relationship to the harvest seasons.

Of the pilgrim festivals, *Pesach* and *Sukkot* are seven-day festivals in the Bible, with the first and last days considered as full days of rest and celebration. *Shavuot* is only a single-day festival. In the Rabbinic period, because of problems in determining the exact dates of the festivals outside the land of Israel, each festival day was kept for two days in the diaspora, a practice still maintained by Orthodox communities but not by Liberal and Reform ones.

GLOSSARY

Abraham Ibn Ezra (1093–1167) – Spanish rabbi, poet, Bible commentator, philosopher and doctor.

Aggadah (Lit., 'Narrative') – All non-legal rabbinic commentary on the Bible.

Amidah (Lit., 'standing') – Central prayer in all Jewish services, consisting of 19 benedictions on weekdays and 7 on Sabbaths and Festivals. Also known as *Shemonei-Esreh* ('eighteen' – the original number of blessings) and *Ha-tefillah* (*the* prayer).

Ashkenazim – Jews from North and Central Europe and their descendants.

Barmitzvah/Batmitzvah – 'Son' (from age 13) or 'Daughter' (from age 12) 'of the Commandment' – from which age they are considered responsible for their actions under Jewish law.

Chanukkah – Festival commemorating the re-dedication of the Temple.

Chasidic – Of Chasidism, a popular pietist and mystical Jewish movement that developed in Eastern Europe in the 18th century.

Chol Ha-Moed – The intermediary days between the first and last full festival days of *Pesach* and *Sukkot*.

Chumash – Hebrew 'five', the 'Five Books of Moses', the *Torah*.

Conservative Judaism – Non-Orthodox religious movement that seeks to preserve Jewish tradition through developing Jewish law.

Edah – Biblical term for the community leadership in the wilderness period.

Haftarah – Reading from the biblical prophetic books for *Shabbat* and Festivals.

Haggadah (Lit., 'Narrative') – The book containing the liturgy for the Passover evening home service.

Halachah – Jewish law.

Hoshana Rabba – Seventh day of the Festival of Sukkot.

Kippah – Skullcap.

Kol Nidre – 'All vows', an aramaic text annulling vows made to God that is chanted on the eve of *Yom Kippur*.

Lag ba-Omer – 33rd day of the Omer period.

Liberal Judaism – Pre-war German non-Orthodox Jewish movement and a more radical British religious movement.

Midrash ('Explanation') – Rabbinic interpretation of either legal (*Midrash Halachah*) or homiletical (*Midrash Aggadah*) character.

Mitzvah (Pl. *Mizvot*) – ('Commandment' or 'precept'). A legal or social obligation incumbent on Jews.

Neder – Biblical term for 'vow'.

Omer – Seven-week period between Passover and Pentecost.

Orthodox Judaism – Term for post-emancipation Judaism that tries to preserve unchanged Jewish tradition, ritual and law.

Parashah – ('Division' Pl. *Parashiot*) – the weekly portion of the Bible read in synagogue. (Also known as *sidra*.)

Pesach – Passover, early spring festival commemorating the Exodus from Egypt.

Purim – A festival celebrating the miraculous deliverance of the Jews recorded in the biblical Book of Esther.

Rashi (Acronym for Rabbi Shlomo Yitzchaki, 1040–1105.) – French rabbi and leading commentator on the Bible and Talmud.

Reconstructionism – American Jewish religious movement, founded by Mordechai Kaplan, that sees Judaism as a religious civilization.

Reform Judaism – A term covering different non-Orthodox Jewish religious movements around the world since the 19th century, from radical (in pre-war Germany) to conservative.

Rosh Chodesh – The beginning, lit 'head', of the month.

Rosh Ha-Shanah – The New (lit. Head of the) Year.

Sefardim – Jews from Spain and Portugal and their descendants.

Shabbat – Sabbath, the seventh day of the week, the day of rest.

Shavuot – The 'Feast of Weeks', Pentecost, late spring festival commemorating the covenant between God and Israel at Mt Sinai.

Shema – 'Hear O Israel …' Three biblical passages (Deuteronomy 6.4–9; 11.13–21; Numbers 15.37–41) recited daily affirming the unity of God and the acceptance of God's commandments.

Shoah – 'Destruction' – Jewish term for the Nazi genocide of the Jews – preferred to the more common term 'Holocaust'.

Shofar – Ram's Horn, blown in the month before and during *Rosh Ha-Shanah* and *Yom Kippur*.

Sidra (Pl. *Sidrot*) – the weekly portion of the Bible read in synagogue, also known as *Parashah*.

Simchat Torah – Rejoicing in the *Torah* – Festival to mark the completion of the annual cycle of weekly Bible readings and beginning again with Genesis.

Sukkot – Tabernacles, autumn harvest festival commemorating the Israelites' wandering in the desert for forty years.

Synagogue – Place for Jewish prayer, study and meeting.

Tallit – Prayer shawl.

Tanchuma – Midrash collection ascribed to Rabbi Tanchuma bar Abba.

Tisha be-Av – Fast on the 'Ninth day of the month of *Av*' commemorating the destruction of the First and Second Temples.

Torah – 'Teaching' – The Five Books of Moses and all derived Jewish teachings.

Tu biShvat – 15th day of the month of Shevat, designated as the New Year for Trees.

Yom Ha-Atzmaut – Israel Independence Day.

Yom Ha-Shoah – 'Day of the Destruction' – memorial day for those murdered by the Nazis during the Second World War.

Yom Kippur – The Day of Atonement.